Remember This?

People, Things and Events
FROM **1942** TO THE **PRESENT DAY**

US EDITION

With thanks for additional research by Larry Farr, Dana Lemay, Rose Myers and Idan Solon.

Cover: Mary Evans: Sueddeutsche Zeitung Photo, The Everett Collection, Keystone Pictures USA/zumapress.com; Library of Congress, HAER CAL,38-SANFRA,141. Icons from rawpixel/Freepik.

Baby statistics: Office of Retirement and Disability Policy, Social Security Administration.

Cover Design: Fanni Williams / thehappycolourstudio.com

The Milestone Memories series including this *Remember This?* title is produced by Milestones Memories Press, a division of Say So Media Ltd.

First edition: October 2021
Updated: February 2022

We've tried our best to check our facts, but mistakes can still slip through. Spotted one? We'd love to know about it: info@saysomedia.net

Rewind, Replay, Remember

What can you remember before you turned six? If you're like most of us, not much: the comforting smell of a blanket or the rough texture of a sweater, perhaps. A mental snapshot of a parent arriving home late at night. A tingle of delight or the shadow of sorrow.

But as we grow out of childhood, our autobiographical and episodic memories—they're the ones hitched to significant events such as birthdays or leaving school—are created and filed more effectively, enabling us to piece them together at a later date. And the more we revisit those memories, the less likely we are to lose the key that unlocks them.

We assemble these fragments into a more-or-less coherent account of our lives—the one we tell to ourselves, our friends, our relatives. And while this one-of-a-kind biopic loses a little definition over the years, some episodes remain in glorious technicolor—although it's usually the most embarrassing incidents!

But this is one movie that's never quite complete. Have you ever had a memory spring back unbidden, triggered by something seemingly unrelated? This book is an attempt to discover those forgotten scenes using the events, sounds, and faces linked to the milestones in your life.

It's time to blow off the cobwebs and see how much you can remember!

It Happened in 1942

The biggest event in the year is one that didn't make the front pages: you were born! Here are some of the national stories that people were talking about.

✦ St. Louis Cardinals win the World Series
✦ Daylight Saving Time goes into effect
✦ Women's Auxiliary Army Corp (WAAC) created
✦ Actor John Barrymore died
✦ War Bonds raise $13 billion
✦ Coffee rationing begins
✦ New car sales banned
✦ FDR signs executive order for internment of Japanese Americans
✦ Fire in the Cocoanut Grove night club kills 492
✦ Bing Crosby records "White Christmas"
✦ Alaska Highway completed
✦ Black Americans enlisted into the US Navy as war begins (right)
✦ Bambi premiers
✦ Casablanca premiers
✦ Voice of America begins broadcasting
✦ FDR orders General Douglas MacArthur out of the Philippines
✦ Gasoline rationing begins
✦ How Green Was My Valley awarded Best Picture
✦ Enrico Fermi initiates first self-sustaining nuclear chain reaction
✦ Actress Carole Lombard is among 22 dead in plane crash

Born this year:
⚭ Boxer Muhammad Ali
⚭ Singer Barbara Streisand
⚭ Actor Harrison Ford
⚭ Businessman Michael Bloomberg

Mary Evans / Sueddeutsche Zeitung Photo

America is on the march: half a million people paraded up Fifth Avenue over 11 hours in June 1942; millions more watched from the sidelines. Next stop for these servicemen was the front.

On the Bookshelf When You Were Small

The books of our childhood linger long in the memory. These are the children's classics, all published in your first ten years. Do you remember the stories? What about the covers?

1942	The Runaway Bunny by Margaret Wise Brown
1942	The Poky Little Puppy by Janette Sebring Lowrey
1943	**The Little Prince by Antoine de Saint-Exupéry** In 1935, poet, aristocrat and aviator de Saint-Exupéry crash-landed in the desert. His hallucinations before eventual rescue were the seeds of the story that would later become the bestseller Le Petit Prince.
1944	Mother Goose by Tasha Tudor
1945	Pippi Longstocking by Astrid Lindgren
1945	Stuart Little by E.B. White
1946	**Thomas the Tank Engine by Rev. W. Awdry** Rev. Awdrey appeared in his own books as the Thin Clergyman. His more portly friend in real life, Teddy Boston, appeared by his fictional side—known, of course, as the Fat Clergyman.
1946	Scuffy the Tugboat by Gertrude Crampton
1946	**The Mystery of the Tolling Bell by Carolyn Keene** The Nancy Drew series ran for 175 books, to 2003. The author of early titles was adventurer journalist Mildred Wirt Benson. She received a flat fee and no recognition until a 1980 court case unraveled her contribution.
1947	Goodnight Moon by Margaret Wise Brown
1948	My Father's Dragon by Ruth Stiles Gannett
1948	Blueberries for Sal by Robert McCloskey
1949	**Bartholomew and the Oobleck by Dr. Seuss** Oobleck is the atrociously gummy substance that rains from the sky in Dr. Seuss's tale, broadly summarized as "be careful what you wish for." Oobleck lives on as the amazing non-Newtonian liquid made from cornstarch.
1950	Better Known as Johnny Appleseed by Mabel Leigh Hunt
1950	The Lion, the Witch and the Wardrobe by C.S. Lewis

Around the World in Your Birth Year

Here are the events from outside the US that were big enough to make news back home in the year you were born. And you won't remember any of them!

+ Rocket reaches space
+ Russia ultimately wins Battle of Stalingrad
+ Declaration of United Nations is signed
+ Singapore surrenders to Japan
+ Thailand declares war on the Allies
+ Coal dust explosion kills over 1500 in China
+ Hitler made "Supreme Judge" as Reichstag dissolved
+ Luxembourg is annexed
+ Anne Frank starts diary
+ Ejector seat is created in Germany
+ Japan attacks Sydney Harbor
+ Princess Elizabeth registers for war service
+ Crisis in Canada over forced conscription
+ Bombs fall on Darwin
+ Concentration camps begin
+ Japan invades Burma
+ Nuclear accident occurs in Germany
+ Hurricane in Bay of Bengal
+ Bombing raids on Tokyo
+ Canada inters citizens of Japanese descent
+ Gandhi is arrested in Bombay
+ Japan forces POWs to make Bataan Death March
+ Vidkun Quisling rules occupied Norway
+ Allied forces win Battle of Midway

Boys' Names When You Were Born

Once upon a time, popular names came... and stuck. (John hogged the top spot for 40 years, to 1924.) These are the most popular names when you were born.

James
James was not only the first choice in 1942, it was the most popular boy's name of the last hundred years, bestowed upon nearly five million babies (narrowly beating John into second place).

Robert
John
William
Richard
David
Charles
Thomas
Ronald
Donald
Joseph
Larry
Michael
George
Kenneth
Jerry
Edward
Gary
Paul
Dennis
Frank
Gerald
Douglas
Raymond

Rising and falling stars:
Leon and Lloyd made their last Top 100 appearance this year. Douglas (23) and Lawrence (31) were never more popular than they were in 1942.

Girls' Names When You Were Born

On the girls' side of the maternity ward, Mary and Helen topped the list for decades. But by 1942, Helen had fallen and Mary's crown was in the balance…

Mary
Mary was the name chosen for 3 million babies over the last century: twice as many as Patricia, the second most popular pick overall.

Barbara
Patricia
Linda
Carol
Sandra
Judith
Nancy
Betty
Carolyn
Tenth place is Carolyn's best ever ranking.

Sharon
Shirley
Joyce
Margaret
Judy
Karen
Dorothy
Joan
Janet
Donna
Susan
Elizabeth
Virginia
Kathleen
Janice

Rising and falling stars:
While Marlene and Edna dropped out of the Top 100, Sheila and Christine were fresh faces.

Things People Did When You Were Growing Up...

...that hardly anyone does now. Some of these we remember fondly; others are best left in the past!

- Help Mom make cookies using a cookie press
- Keep bread in a breadbox
- Can and preserve vegetables from your garden
- Listen to daytime soap operas on the radio
- Participate in Church fundraisers
- Watch endurance competitions like flagpole sitting and goldfish eating
- Build scooters from roller skates and scrap wood
- Bring a slide-rule to math class
- Take a Sunday drive out to the country
- Play leapfrog
- Live in a Sears Modern Home ordered from the Sears catalog
- Get a treat from the pharmacy soda fountain
- Camp in a "Hooverville" while looking for work
- Keep a thrift or kitchen garden
- Buy penny candy
- Buy goods from door-to-door salesmen
- Wear clothing made from flour sacks
- Collect marbles
- Join a dance marathon
- Listen to Amos n' Andy on the radio on weekend evenings
- Eat Water Pie
- "Window shop" downtown on Saturdays
- Pitch pennies
- Earn $30 a month plus food and shelter working for the Civilian Conservation Corps

How Many of These Games Are Still Played?

The first half of the 20th century was the heyday for new board and card games launched to the US public. Some are still firm family favorites, but which ones did you play when you were young?

1925	Pegity
1925	Playing for the Cup
1927	Hokum ("The game for a roomful")
1920s	The Greyhound Racing Game
1930	Wahoo
1932	Finance
1934	Sorry!
1935	**Monopoly** The game's origins lie with The Landlord's Game, patented in 1904 by Elizabeth Magie. (The anti-monopoly version—Prosperity—didn't catch on.) It was the first game with a never-ending path rather than a fixed start and finish.
1935	Easy Money
1936	The Amazing Adventures of Fibber McGee
1937	Meet the Missus
1937	Stock Ticker
1938	Scrabble
1938	Movie Millions
1940	Dig
1940	Prowl Car
1942	Sea Raider
1943	Chutes and Ladders
1949	**Clue** Clue—or Cluedo, as it is known to most outside the USA—introduced us to a host of shady characters and grisly murder weapons. For years those included a piece of genuine lead pipe, now replaced on health grounds.
1949	**Candy Land** This wholesome family racing game, invented on a polio ward, was the victim of something less savory nearly 50 years after its launch when an adult website claimed the domain name. Thankfully, the courts swiftly intervened.

Things People Do Now...

...that were virtually unknown when you were young.
How many of these habits are part of your routine or even
second nature these days? Do you remember the first time?

- ✦ Get curbside grocery pickup
- ✦ Stream movies instead of going to Blockbuster for a rental
- ✦ Learn remotely and online
- ✦ Communicate by text or video chat
- ✦ Use a Kindle or other e-reading device
- ✦ Go geocaching
- ✦ Track your sleep, exercise, or fertility with a watch
- ✦ Use a weighted blanket
- ✦ Use a robotic/automatic vacuum
- ✦ Take your dog to a dog park
- ✦ Have a package delivered by drone
- ✦ Find a date online or through an app
- ✦ Use hand sanitizer
- ✦ Automatically soothe your baby with a self-rocking bassinet
- ✦ Host a gender-reveal party during pregnancy
- ✦ Use a home essential oil diffuser or salt lamp
- ✦ Have a "destination wedding"
- ✦ Use a device charging station while waiting for a flight
- ✦ Get a ride from Uber or Lyft instead of a taxi
- ✦ Drink hard seltzer
- ✦ Take a home DNA test (for you... or your pet)
- ✦ Have a telemedicine/virtual healthcare visit
- ✦ Smoke an e-cigarette/"vape"
- ✦ Start your car, dryer, or air conditioner via an app

Popular Food in the 1950s

For many, the post-war years meant more of one thing in particular on the table: meat. In the yard, men stepped up to the barbeque to sharpen their skills. In the kitchen, fancy new electric appliances and frozen TV dinners promised convenience and new, exotic flavors.

Tuna noodle casserole

Dinty Moore Beef Stew

Beef stroganoff

Green bean casserole

Green bean casserole was invented in the Campbell's test kitchen in 1955 as a cheap, fuss-free dish. Today, around 40 percent of Campbell's Cream of Mushroom soup sold in the US goes into this dinner table staple.

Pigs-in-a-blanket

Pigs get different blankets in the United Kingdom, where sausages are wrapped in bacon rather than pastry.

Backyard barbecues

Ovaltine

Swedish meatballs

Pineapple upside down cake

Spam

Ground pork shoulder and ham sold in a distinctive can—for much of the world, that means Spam. This "meatloaf without basic training" is affordable and still popular, with over eight billion cans sold since it was first sold in 1937.

Ambrosia salad

Sugar Smacks

Cheez Whiz

Stuffed celery

Campbell's Tomato Soup spice cake

Swanson Turkey TV Dinners

Dreamed up as a solution to an over-supply of turkey, TV dinners proved nearly as popular as the TV itself. Swanson sold over 25 million of them in 1954, the year these handy meal packs were launched.

Veg-All canned vegetables

Chicken à la King

Cars of the 1950s

Was this the golden age of automobiles? In truth, some of these models had been brought to market long before, such as the Buick Roadmaster and the Studebaker Champion. But even stalwarts were quick to adopt the Space Age theme of the decade as sweeping lines, tailfins, and cascading chrome grilles became the norm.

1926	Chrysler Imperial
1936	General Motors Buick Roadmaster
1939	**Studebaker Champion** Over seven decades, the Champion's creator, Raymond Loewy, designed railroads, logos, buses, vending machines, and a space station for NASA.
1939	Chrysler DeSoto Custom
1947	Studebaker Starlight Coupe
1948	**Crosley Station Wagon** The first car to be marketed as "Sports Utility."
1948	Jaguar XK120
1949	**Muntz Jet** Fewer than 200 Muntz Jets were built by founder Madman Muntz, an engineer who married seven times and made (and lost) fortunes selling cars, TVs, and more.
1949	Chrysler Dodge Coronet
1950	General Motors Chevrolet Bel-Air
1950	Nash Rambler
1951	Hudson Hornet
1953	General Motors Chevrolet Corvette
1953	General Motors Buick Skylark
1953	General Motors Cadillac Eldorado
1953	Nash Metropolitan
1954	Ford Skyliner
1955	Ford Thunderbird
1955	Ford Fairlane
1956	Studebaker Golden Hawk
1956	Chrysler Plymouth Fury
1957	**Mercedes-Benz 300 SL Roadster** Voted "Sports Car of the Century" in 1999.

Cars crawl out of 1950s Philadelphia over the Ben Franklin Bridge. Henry Ford wasn't the only one to "build a car for the great multitude." Millions of new suburbanites embraced their newfound freedom—even if that meant driving to the same place as everyone else.

The Biggest Hits When You Were 10

Whistled by your father, hummed by your sister or overheard on the radio, these are the hit records as you reached double digits.

Percy Faith 🎵 Delicado

The Dominoes 🎵 Have Mercy Baby

Kay Starr 🎵 Wheel of Fortune

The Weavers 🎵 Wimoweh

B.B. King 🎵 3 O'Clock Blues

Al Martino 🎵 Here in My Heart

Jo Stafford 🎵 You Belong to Me

Hank Thompson & His Brazo Valley Boys 🎵 The Wild Side of Life

Eddie Boyd 🎵 Five Long Years

Leroy Anderson 🎵 Blue Tango

Hank Williams 🎵 Jambalaya (On the Bayou)

Lloyd Price 🎵 Lawdy Miss Clawdy

Patti Page 🎵 I Went to Your Wedding

Vera Lynn 🎵 Auf Wiederseh'n, Sweetheart

Slim Willet with the Brush Cutters 🎵 Don't Let the Stars (Get in Your Eyes)

Little Walter 🎵 Juke

Georgia Gibbs 🎵 Kiss of Fire

Frankie Laine 🎵 High Noon (Do Not Forsake Me)

Rosemary Clooney 🎵 Botch-A-Me (Ba-Ba-Baciami Piccina)

Kitty Wells 🎵 It Wasn't God Who Made Honky Tonk Angels

Carl Smith 🎵 (When You Feel Like You're in Love) Don't Just Stand There

Doris Day 🎵 A Guy Is a Guy

Ruth Brown 🎵 5-10-15 Hours

Jimmy Boyd 🎵 I Saw Mommy Kissing Santa Claus

Faster, Easier, Better

Yesterday's technological breakthrough is today's modern convenience. Here are some of the lab and engineering marvels that were made before you turned 21 years old.

1942	**Toilet paper** Until 1942, the best you could hope for from your toilet paper was that it was splinter-free. But in a big boost to their bottom line, a paper mill in England began to offer two-ply toilet paper for a softer touch.
1943	Kidney dialysis machine
1944	Programmable calculator
1945	Cruise control in cars
1946	**Waterproof diaper** The inventor of the first waterproof diaper, the Boater, was told repeatedly that no one wanted it and no one had been asking for such a thing. She decided to manufacture it herself and the product was an immediate success.
1947	Transistor
1948	Computer program
1949	Wurlitzer Select-O-Matic jukebox
1949	Zamboni ice resurfacer
1950	Teleprompter
1951	Wetsuit
1952	Artificial heart
1953	Heart-lung machine
1954	Acoustic suspension loudspeaker
1955	Pocket transistor radio
1956	Hard Disk Drive
1956	Operating system (OS)
1957	Laser
1958	Microchip
1959	Weather satellite
1960	Global navigation satellite system
1961	Spreadsheet (electronic)
1962	Red LED

Across the Nation

10

Double digits at last: you're old enough to eavesdrop on adults and scan the headlines. These may be some of the earliest national news stories you remember.

+ Mechanical heart used in a human patient
+ Truman announces he will not seek reelection
+ Richard Nixon's "Checkers" speech
+ Computer UNIVAC correctly predicts presidential election
+ Dwight Eisenhower elected president
+ Boxer Floyd Patterson wins gold
+ Black umpire hired in Major League Baseball
+ Mr. Potato Head toy offered for sale
+ Bob Mathias wins 2nd gold for decathlon
+ Skier Andrea Mead-Lawrence becomes only multi-gold winner
+ Plastic lenses for cataract patients used
+ Truman seizes steel mills to avert strike
+ Braves leave Boston
+ Charlie Chaplin banned from US
+ Jonas Salk develops polio vaccine
+ Maureen Connolly wins Wimbledon and US Open
+ Boxer Rocky Marciano becomes Heavyweight Champion
+ Ban on the "panic-inducing" word tornado lifted
+ Automated pinsetter approved by American Bowling Congress
+ Plane lands on North Pole
+ SS United States sets new time record crossing the Atlantic
+ Queen Juliana of the Netherlands speaks to Congress
+ Secretary's Day celebrated
+ Helicopter flies over the Atlantic

Born this year:
- Actor Patrick Swayze
- Actor Mickey Rourke
- Comedian Roseanne Barr

Kapow! Comic Books and Heroes from Your Childhood

Barely a year went past in the mid-20th Century without a new super-powered hero arriving to save the day. Here are some that were taking on the bad guys during your childhood.

All Star Comics ✷ Justice Society of America
Sensation Comics ✷ Wonder Woman
Mickey Mouse ✷ Mickey Mouse
The Flash ✷ Jay Garrick
Adventure Comics ✷ Aquaman
Venus ✷ Venus
Casper The Friendly Ghost ✷ Casper
Strange Adventures ✷ Captain Comet
Donald Duck ✷ Donald Duck
Uncle Scrooge ✷ Uncle Scrooge
Phantom Stranger ✷ Phantom Stranger
Action Comics ✷ Superman
Detective Comics ✷ Batman
Rawhide Kid ✷ Rawhide Kid
Showcase ✷ Barry Allen
World's Finest Comics ✷ Superman
Patsy Walker ✷ Patsy Walker
Kid Colt, Outlaw ✷ Kid Colt

Winners of the Stanley Cup Since You Were Born

The prestigious Stanley Cup has been changing hands since 1893, although the trophy itself has been redesigned more than once. Here are the teams to lift the champagne-filled cup since you were born.

- **Detroit Red Wings (9)**
  1955: 18-year-old Larry Hillman became the youngest player to have his name engraved on the Stanley Cup trophy.
- Chicago Black Hawks (4)
- **Boston Bruins (3)**
  1970: Bobby Orr scored perhaps the most famous goal in NHL history, in midair, to clinch the title.
- **New York Rangers (1)**
  After a 1940 victory, the Rangers would not win another Stanley Cup for another 54 years.
- Toronto Maple Leafs (10)
- Montreal Canadiens (20)
- Philadelphia Flyers (2)
- New York Islanders (4)
- Edmonton Oilers (5)
- **Calgary Flames (1)**
  1989 was the last time a Stanley Cup Final has been played between two teams from Canada.
- Pittsburgh Penguins (5)
- New Jersey Devils (3)
- **Colorado Avalanche (2)**
  1996: A win in their first season after moving from Quebec (where their nickname was the Nordiques).
- Dallas Stars (1)
- Tampa Bay Lightning (3)
- Carolina Hurricanes (1)
- Anaheim Ducks (1)
- Los Angeles Kings (2)
- Washington Capitals (1)
- St. Louis Blues (1)

On the Silver Screen When You Were 11

From family favorites to the films you weren't allowed to watch, these are the films and actors that drew the praise and the crowds when you turned 11.

Peter Pan 🎞 Bobby Driscoll, Hans Conried, Kathryn Beaumont

Niagara 🎞 Marilyn Monroe, Joseph Cotten, Jean Peters

Shane 🎞 Alan Ladd, Jean Arthur, Van Heflin

House of Wax 🎞 Vincent Price, Frank Lovejoy, Phyllis Kirk

Pickup on South Street 🎞 Richard Widmark, Jean Peters, Thelma Ritter

The Beast from 20,000 Fathoms 🎞 Paul Christian, Paula Raymond, Cecil Kellaway

It Came from Outer Space 🎞 Charles Drake, Joe Sawyer, Russell Johnson

Gentlemen Prefer Blondes 🎞 Marilyn Monroe, Jane Russell

From Here to Eternity 🎞 Burt Lancaster, Montgomery Clift, Frank Sinatra

The Robe 🎞 Richard Burton, Jean Simmons, Victor Mature

How to Marry a Millionaire 🎞 Betty Grable, Marilyn Monroe, Lauren Bacall

Calamity Jane 🎞 Doris Day, Howard Keel, Allyn Ann McLerie

Hondo 🎞 John Wayne, Geraldine Page, Ward Bond
The filming ran over schedule and director John Farrow left production, leaving John Ford to direct the final scenes.

House of Wax 🎞 Vincent Price, Frank Lovejoy, Phyllis Kirk

I Confess 🎞 Montgomery Clift, Anne Baxter, Karl Malden
Director Alfred Hitchcock became frustrated with Montgomery Clift's method acting, having him repeat take after take.

Julius Caesar 🎞 Marlon Brando, James Mason, John Gielgud

The Band Wagon 🎞 Fred Astaire, Cyd Charisse, Oscar Levant

Roman Holiday 🎞 Gregory Peck, Audrey Hepburn, Eddie Albert

The Wild One 🎞 Marlon Brando, Mary Murphy, Robert Keith

The War of the Worlds 🎞 Gene Barry, Ann Robinson, Lewis Martin

Stalag 17 🎞 William Holden, Otto Preminger, Don Taylor

The Big Heat 🎞 Glenn Ford, Gloria Grahame, Jocelyn Brando

Angel Face 🎞 Robert Mitchum, Jean Simmons, Mona Freeman

Comic Strips You'll Know

Comic strips took off in the late 19th century and for much of the 20th century they were a dependable feature of everyday life. Some were solo efforts; others became so-called zombie strips, living on well beyond their creator. A century on, some are still going. But how many from your youth will you remember?

1940–52	The Spirit by Will Eisner
1930–	**Blondie** In 1995, Blondie was one of 20 strips commemorated by the US Postal Service in the Comic Strip Classics series.
1931–	**Dick Tracy** Gould's first idea? A detective called Plainclothes Tracy.
1930–95	Mickey Mouse
1932–	Mary Worth
1936–	**The Phantom** Lee Falk worked on The Phantom for 63 years and Mandrake The Magician for 65.
1919–	Barney Google and Snuffy Smith
1938–	Nancy
1946–	Mark Trail
1937–	**Prince Valiant** Edward, the Duke of Windsor (previously Edward VIII), called Prince Valiant the "greatest contribution to English literature in the past hundred years."
1934–2003	**Flash Gordon** Alex Raymond created Flash Gordon to compete with the Buck Rogers comic strip.
1934–77	Li'l Abner by Al Capp
1925–74	Etta Kett by Paul Robinson
1947–69	Grandma by Charles Kuhn
1948–	Rex Morgan, M.D.
1933–87	Brick Bradford
1950–2000	**Peanuts by Charles M. Schulz** Schultz was inducted into the Hockey Hall of Fame after building the Redwood Empire Arena near his studio.
1950–	Beetle Bailey

Biggest Hits by The King

He may have conquered rock'n'roll, but Elvis's success straddled genres including country music, R&B, and more. These are his Number 1s from across the charts, beginning with the rockabilly "I Forgot..." through the posthumous country hit, "Guitar Man."

I Forgot to Remember to Forget (1955)
Heartbreak Hotel (1956)
I Want You, I Need You, I Love You (1956)
Don't Be Cruel (1956)
Hound Dog (1956)
Love Me Tender (1956)
Too Much (1957)
All Shook Up (1957)
(Let Me Be Your) Teddy Bear (1957)
Jailhouse Rock (1957)
Don't (1957)
Wear My Ring Around Your Neck (1958)
Hard Headed Woman (1958)
A Big Hunk O' Love (1959)
Stuck On You (1960)
It's Now or Never (1960)
Are You Lonesome Tonight? (1960)
Surrender (1961)
Good Luck Charm (1962)
Suspicious Minds (1969)
Moody Blue (1976)
Way Down (1977)
Guitar Man (1981)

Childhood Candies

In labs across the country, mid-century food scientists dreamed up new and colorful ways to delight children just like you. These are the fruits of their labor, launched before you turned twenty-one.

1945	Dots (Mason Company)
1946	Almond Joy (Peter Paul)
1947	Bazooka Bubble Gum (Topps Candy Company)
1949	Jolly Rancher (Jolly Rancher Company)
1949	Junior Mints (James O. Welch Company)
1949	**Whoppers** (Overland Candy Company) Whoppers were known as "Giants" before 1949.
1949	Smarties (Ce De Candy, Inc.)
1950	Cup-O-Gold (Hoffman Candy Company)
1950	Red Vines (American Licorice Co.)
1950	Hot Tamales (Just Born)
1950	Rocky Road Candy Bar (The Annabell Candy Co.)
1952	Pixy Stix (Sunline, Inc.)
1954	Atomic Fireballs (Ferrera Candy Co.)
1954	**Marshmallow Peeps** (Just Born) Today it takes six minutes to make one Peep, but when the candy was first introduced, it took 27 hours!
1954	Peanut M&Ms (Mars)
1955	**Chick-O-Sticks** (Atkinson's) These candies were called "Chicken Bones" until they were renamed in 1955.
1950s	Swedish Fish (Malaco)
1950s	Look! Candy Bar (Golden Nugget Candy Co.)
1960	Sixlets (Leaf Brands)
1962	Now and Later (Phoenix Candy Company)
1962	**SweeTarts** (Sunline, Inc.) These have the same candy base as Pixy Stix which was invented using drink powder from a children's drink.
1962	LemonHead (Ferrara Candy Company)

Books of the Decade

Ten years of your life that took you from adventure books aged 10 to dense works of profundity at 20—or perhaps just grown-up adventures! How many did you read when they were first published?

1952	Invisible Man by Ralph Ellison
1952	The Old Man and the Sea by Ernest Hemingway
1952	East of Eden by John Steinbeck
1953	Fahrenheit 451 by Ray Bradbury
1953	The Adventures of Augie March by Saul Bellow
1954	The Fellowship of the Ring by J.R.R. Tolkien
1954	Under the Net by Iris Murdoch
1955	Lolita by Vladimir Nabokov
1955	The Ginger Man by J.P. Donleavy
1955	The Two Towers by J.R.R. Tolkien
1956	Peyton Place by Grace Metalious
1956	Giovanni's Room by James Baldwin
1956	The Return of the King by J.R.R. Tolkien
1957	On the Road by Jack Kerouac
1957	Atlas Shrugged by Ayn Rand
1958	Breakfast at Tiffany's by Truman Capote
1958	Doctor Zhivago by Boris Pasternak
1958	Exodus by Leon Uris
1959	The Haunting of Hill House by Shirley Jackson
1959	Naked Lunch by William S. Burroughs
1959	Advise and Consent by Allen Drury
1960	To Kill a Mockingbird by Harper Lee
1960	Hawaii by James Michener
1961	Catch-22 by Joseph Heller
1961	Stranger in a Strange Land by Robert A. Heinlein

US Buildings

Some were loathed then, loved now; others, the reverse. Some broke new architectural ground; others housed famous or infamous businesses, or helped to power a nation. All of them were built in your first 18 years.

1942	New Frontier Hotel and Casino, Las Vegas
1943	The Pentagon
1944	Geneva Steel Mill, Utah
1945	Pacific Gas and Electric Company General Office Building and Annex, SF
1946	**Flamingo Hotel, Las Vegas** The Presidential Suite at The Flamingo originally featured a few extras by request of its mobster owner, "Bugsy" Siegel: bulletproof glass and a secret escape ladder. Siegel was shot dead in Beverly Hills.
1947	75 Rockefeller Plaza
1948	Mile High Stadium, Denver
1949	Promontory Apartments, Chicago
1950	Metropolitan Life North Building
1951	US General Accounting Office Building
1952	United Nations Secretariat Building
1953	Sullivan Tower, Nashville
1954	Republic Center, Dallas
1955	One Prudential Plaza, Chicago
1956	**Capitol Records Building, Los Angeles** The world's first circular office building.
1957	666 Fifth Avenue, New York City
1958	Time & Life Building, New York City
1959	2 Broadway, New York City
1960	Four Gateway Center, Pittsburgh

Radio DJs from Your Childhood

If the radio was the soundtrack to your life as you grew up, some of these voices were part of the family. (The stations listed are where these DJs made their name; the dates are their radio broadcasting career).

Wolfman Jack 🎤 XERB/Armed Forces Radio (1960–1995)

Jocko Henderson 🎤 WDAS/W LIB (1952–1991)

Casey Kasem 🎤 KRLA (1954–2010)
Kasem was the host of American Top 40 for four decades. By 1986, his show was broadcast on 1,000 radio stations.

Bruce Morrow 🎤 WABC (1959-)

Murray Kaufman 🎤 WINS (1958–1975)
You'll likely remember him as Murray the K, the self-declared "fifth Beatle" (he played a lot of music from the Fab Four).

Alison Steele 🎤 WNEW-FM (1966–1995)
Aka The Nightbird, Steele was that rarity of the sixties and seventies: a successful female DJ.

Alan Freed 🎤 WJW/WINS (1945–1965)
Freed's career crashed after he was found to have been taking payola. His contribution was recognized posthumously when admitted into the Rock n Roll Hall of Fame.

Robert W. Morgan 🎤 KHJ-AM (1955–1998)

Dan Ingram 🎤 WABC (1958–2004)

Dave Hull 🎤 KRLA (1955–2010)
Another candidate for the "fifth Beatle," Hull interviewed the band many times.

Hal Jackson 🎤 WBLS (1940–2011)

Johnny Holliday 🎤 KYA (1956-)

Herb Kent 🎤 WVON (1944–2016)
"Cool Gent" Herb Kent was the longest-serving DJ on the radio.

Tom Donahue 🎤 WIBG/KYA (1949–1975)

John R. 🎤 WLAC (1941–1973)

Bill Randle 🎤 WERE/WCBS (1940s-2004)

Jack Spector 🎤 WMCA (1955–1994)
Spector, one of WMCA's "Good Guys," died on air in 1994. A long silence after playing "I'm in the Mood for Love" alerted station staff.

It Happened in 1958

Here's a round-up of the most newsworthy events from across the US in the year you turned (sweet) 16.

✦ Flag with 50 stars designed by junior high student
✦ Singer Jerry Lee Lewis sparks controversy with marriage to child relative
✦ Charles Starkweather goes on a killing spree
✦ Radio's "Payola" scandal breaks
✦ Actress Lana Turner's boyfriend killed by her teenage daughter in justifiable homicide
✦ Frank Lloyd Wright designs his only gas station project
✦ Record-setting tsunami hits Alaska
✦ Worst ever school bus tragedy kills 26 in Kentucky
✦ American Express card introduced
✦ Superglue sold
✦ Hula Hoops hit the market
✦ "Look Ma, no cavities!" ad created
✦ Bank of America begins a program that becomes the Visa Card
✦ Crayola renames Prussian Blue to Midnight Blue
✦ Mr. Clean gets to work
✦ Candy necklaces go on sale
✦ Pizza Hut founded
✦ New York Yankees win the World Series
✦ Last battleship decommissioned
✦ Vanguard I satellite launched
✦ Two servicemen are laid in the Tomb of the Unknown Soldiers
✦ Singer Elvis Presley inducted into the US Army (right)

Born this year:
♊ Singers Prince, Madonna, and Michael Jackson
♊ Actor Kevin Bacon
♊ Rapper Ice T

Mary Evans / The Everett Collection

In 1958, many parents and teachers, long concerned about the pernicious effect of rock'n'roll, sighed with relief. Elvis would serve as a regular soldier. Behind the scenes, the singer's agent gave him little choice. Joining the Special Services—an option that would have seen Elvis avoid service in return for concerts—meant giving away worldwide royalties, and wouldn't prove popular with the public in any case. He was in a "funny position," as he would later say. His fate was sealed, and on March 24, he reported for duty.

Elvis's early army life was scarred by homesickness and the death of his mother, aged 46, from a heart attack. The following month, Elvis was posted to West

News Anchors of the Fifties and Sixties

Trusted, familiar, and exclusively male: these are the faces that brought you the news, and the catchphrases they made their own.

Edward R. Murrow 📺 CBS (1938-59)
"Good night, and good luck."

Walter Cronkite 📺 CBS (1962-81)
"And that's the way it is."

David Brinkley 📺 NBC (1956-71)
"Good night, Chet..."

Chet Huntley 📺 NBC (1956-70)
"...Good night, David."

Harry Reasoner 📺 CBS & ABC (1961-91)

Frank Reynolds 📺 ABC (1968-70)

John Charles Daly 📺 CBS & ABC (1941-60)
"Good night and a good tomorrow."

Douglas Edwards 📺 CBS (1948-62)

Hugh Downs 📺 NBC (1962-71)

John Chancellor 📺 NBC (1970-82)

Paul Harvey 📺 ABC Radio (1951-2009)
"Hello Americans, this is Paul Harvey. Stand by for news!"

Mike Wallace 📺 CBS (1963-66)

John Cameron Swayze 📺 NBC (1948-56)
"Well, that's the story, folks! This is John Cameron Swayze, and I'm glad we could get together."

Ron Cochran 📺 ABC (1962-65)

Bob Young 📺 ABC (1967-68)

Dave Garroway 📺 NBC (1952-61)

Bill Shadel 📺 ABC (1960-63)

Fifties Game Shows

It all started so well: appointment radio became appointment TV, with new and crossover game shows bringing us together. But as the decade progressed, the scandal emerged: some shows were fixed. Quiz shows were down, but certainly not out. (Dates include periods off-air.)

Break the Bank 🎙 (1945–57)

Beat The Clock 🎙 (1950–2019)

Name That Tune 🎙 (1952–85)
A radio crossover that spawned 25 international versions.

Strike It Rich 🎙 (1947–58)

The Price Is Right 🎙 (1956–65)
The original version of the current quiz that began in 1972. This one was hosted by Bill Cullen.

Down You Go 🎙 (1951–56)

I've Got A Secret 🎙 (1952–2006)

What's The Story 🎙 (1951–55)

The $64,000 Question 🎙 (1955–58)

People Are Funny 🎙 (1942–60)

Tic-Tac-Dough 🎙 (1956–90)
Early Tic-Tac-Dough contestants were often coached; around three-quarters of the shows in one run were rigged.

The Name's The Same 🎙 (1951–55)

Two For The Money 🎙 (1952–57)

The Big Payoff 🎙 (1951–62)

Twenty-One 🎙 (1956–58)
At the heart of the rigging scandal, Twenty-One was the subject of Robert Redford's 1994 movie, Quiz Show.

Masquerade Party 🎙 (1952–60)

You Bet Your Life 🎙 (1947–61)
A comedy quiz hosted by Groucho Marx.

Truth or Consequences 🎙 (1940–88)
Started life as a radio quiz. TV host Bob Barker signed off with: "Hoping all your consequences are happy ones."

20 Questions 🎙 (1946–55)

What's My Line 🎙 (1950–75)

Liberty Issue Stamps

First released in 1954, the Liberty Issue drew its name from not one but three depictions of the Statue of Liberty across the denominations. (There was only room for one "real" woman, though.) It coincided with the new era of stamp collecting as a childhood hobby that endured for decades. Were you one of these new miniature philatelists?

Benjamin Franklin ½ ¢ 🖾 Polymath (writer, inventor, scientist)
**Franklin discovered the principle of electricity,
the Law of Conservation of Charge.**

George Washington 1 ¢ 🖾 First US President
Palace of the Governors 1 ¼ ¢ 🖾
**A building in Santa Fe, New Mexico that served as
the seat of government of New Mexico for centuries.**

Mount Vernon 1 ½ ¢ 🖾 George Washington's plantation
Thomas Jefferson 2 ¢ 🖾 Polymath; third US President
Bunker Hill Monument 2 ½ ¢ 🖾 Battle site of the Revolutionary War
Statue of Liberty 3 ¢ 🖾 Gifted by the people of France
Abraham Lincoln 4 ¢ 🖾 16th US President
**Lincoln received a patent for a flotation device that assisted
boats in moving through shallow water.**

The Hermitage 4 ½ ¢ 🖾 Andrew Jackson's plantation
James Monroe 5 ¢ 🖾 Fifth US President
Theodore Roosevelt 6 ¢ 🖾 26th US President
Woodrow Wilson 7 ¢ 🖾 28th US President; served during WW1
John J. Pershing 8 ¢ 🖾 US Army officer during World War I
Alamo 9 ¢ 🖾 Site of a pivotal Texas Revolution battle
Independence Hall 10 ¢ 🖾 Independence declared here
Benjamin Harrison 12 ¢ 🖾 23rd US President
John Jay 15 ¢ 🖾 First Chief Justice of the United States
Monticello 20 ¢ 🖾 Thomas Jefferson's plantation
Paul Revere 25 ¢ 🖾 Alerted militia of the British approach
Robert E. Lee 30 ¢ 🖾 Confederate general in the Civil War
John Marshall 40 ¢ 🖾 Fourth Chief Justice of the US
Susan B. Anthony 50 ¢ 🖾 Women's suffrage activist
Patrick Henry $1 🖾 Leader of the Dec. of Independence
Alexander Hamilton $5 🖾 First Secretary of the Treasury

The Biggest Hits When You Were 16

The artists that topped the charts when you turned 16 might not be in your top 10 these days, but you'll probably remember them!

Chuck Berry 🎸 Johnny B. Goode
Sheb Wooley 🎸 Purple People Eater
Little Richard 🎸 Good Golly, Miss Molly
Perry Como 🎸 Catch a Falling Star
The Chantels 🎸 Maybe
Ritchie Valens 🎸 La Bamba
The Everly Brothers 🎸 All I Have to Do Is Dream
Conway Twitty 🎸 It's Only Make Believe
The Coasters 🎸 Yakety Yak
The Monotones 🎸 Book of Love
Johnny Cash 🎸 Guess Things Happen That Way
Bobby Day 🎸 Rockin' Robin
The Silhouettes 🎸 Get a Job
Perez Prado and His Orchestra 🎸 Patricia
The Kingston Trio 🎸 Tom Dooley
Bobby Darin 🎸 Splish Splash
The Teddy Bears 🎸 To Know Him Is to Love Him
Marty Robbins 🎸 The Story of My Life
Big Bopper 🎸 Chantilly Lace
The Champs 🎸 Tequila
The McGuire Sisters 🎸 Sugartime
Sam Cooke 🎸 I'll Come Running Back to You
The Crests 🎸 Sixteen Candles
The Platters 🎸 Twilight Time

Medical Advances Before You Were 21

A baby born in 1920 USA had a life expectancy of just 55.4 years. By 2000 that was up to 76.8, thanks to medical advances including many of these.

1942	Mechlorethamine chemotherapy
1943	Kidney dialysis
1944	Disposable catheter
1944	Asperger syndrome (described)
1945	Oral penicillin
1946	All-glass syringe (easier sterilization)
1947	Defibrillation
1948	Acetaminophen
1949	Intraocular lens (myopia and cataracts)
1950	**Polio vaccine** Jonas Salk was asked about taking a patent on the polio vaccine. He replied, "Can you patent the sun?"
1951	Munchhausen syndrome (described)
1952	Cloning
1953	Ultrasound
1954	Kidney transplant
1955	Mass immunization of polio
1956	**Metered-dose inhaler** Invented after the teen daughter of head of Riker Labs asked why her asthma medicine couldn't be in a can like hair spray. At the time, asthma medicine was given in ineffective squeeze bulb glass containers.
1957	EEG topography (toposcope)
1958	Pacemaker
1959	Bone marrow transplant
1959	In vitro fertilization
1960	CPR
1960	The pill
1960	Coronary artery bypass surgery
1962	Hip replacement
1962	Beta blocker

Blockbuster Movies When You Were 16

These are the movies that everyone was talking about. How many of them did you see (or have you seen since)?

Gigi 🎬 Leslie Caron, Louis Jourdan, Maurice Chevalier

South Pacific 🎬 Rossano Brazzi, Mitzi Gaynor, John Kerr
The soundtrack was #1 on the Billboard 200 in the US for seven months, the fourth longest run ever.

Marjorie Morningstar 🎬 Gene Kelly, Natalie Wood, Claire Trevor

Vertigo 🎬 James Stewart, Kim Novak, Tom Helmore

Touch of Evil 🎬 Charlton Heston, Janet Leigh, Joseph Calleia

The Bravados 🎬 Gregory Peck, Lee Van Cleef, Stephen Boyd

Indiscreet 🎬 Cary Grant, Ingrid Bergman, Cecil Parker

The Big Country 🎬 Gregory Peck, Jean Simmons, Charlton Heston

Cat on a Hot Tin Roof 🎬 Elizabeth Taylor, Paul Newman, Burl Ives
A week into production, Elizabeth Taylor contracted a virus that caused her to cancel plans to fly to New York where her husband was to receive an honor. The plane crashed.

I Want to Live! 🎬 Susan Hayward, Simon Oakland

The Inn of the
Sixth Happiness 🎬 Ingrid Bergman, Curt Jurgens, Robert Donat

Auntie Mame 🎬 Rosalind Russell, Forrest Tucker, Coral Browne

Separate Tables 🎬 Rita Hayworth, Deborah Kerr, David Niven

The Defiant Ones 🎬 Tony Curtis, Sidney Poitier, Theodore Bikel

Some Came Running 🎬 Frank Sinatra, Dean Martin, Shirley MacLaine

Man of the West 🎬 Gary Cooper, Julie London, Lee J. Cobb

Horror of Dracula 🎬 Peter Cushing, Michael Gough, Melissa Stribling

The Vikings 🎬 Kirk Douglas, Tony Curtis, Janet Leigh

Windjammer (doc.) 🎬 Niels Arntsen, Erik Bye, Pablo Casals

Run Silent Run Deep 🎬 Burt Lancaster, Clark Gable, Jack Warden

King Creole 🎬 Elvis Presley, Carolyn Jones, Walter Matthau

The Blob 🎬 Steve McQueen, Earl Rowe, Aneta Corsaut

Game Show Hosts of the Fifties and Sixties

Many of these men were semi-permanent fixtures, their voices and catchphrases ringing through the decades. Some were full-time entertainers; others were on sabbatical from more serious news duties.

John Charles Daly ➤➤ What's My Line (1950-67)

Art Linkletter ➤➤ People Are Funny (1943-60)

Garry Moore ➤➤ I've Got A Secret (1956-64)

Groucho Marx ➤➤ You Bet Your Life (1949-61)

Warren Hull ➤➤ Strike It Rich (1947-58)

Herb Shriner ➤➤ Two For The Money (1952-56)

George DeWitt ➤➤ Name That Tune (1953-59)

Robert Q. Lewis ➤➤ Name's The Same (1951-54)

Bill Cullen ➤➤ The Price Is Right (1956-65)

Walter Cronkite ➤➤ It's News To Me (1954)
"The most trusted man in America" was briefly the host of this topical quiz game. He didn't do it again.

Bill Slater ➤➤ 20 Questions (1949-52)

Walter Kiernan ➤➤ Who Said That (1951-54)

Bob Eubanks ➤➤ The Newlywed Game (1966-74)

Bud Collyer ➤➤ To Tell The Truth (1956-69)

Jack Barry ➤➤ Twenty-One (1956-58)

Bert Parks ➤➤ Break The Bank (1945-57)

Hugh Downs ➤➤ Concentration (1958-69)

Mike Stokey ➤➤ Pantomime Quiz (1947-59)

Allen Ludden ➤➤ Password (1961-75)

Bob Barker ➤➤ Truth or Consequences (1956-74)
Barker also spent 35 years hosting The Price Is Right.

Hal March ➤➤ $64,000 Question (1955-58)

Monty Hall ➤➤ Let's Make A Deal (1963-91)
Monty—born "Monte", but misspelled on an early publicity photo—was also a philanthropist who raised around $1 billion over his lifetime.

Johnny Carson ➤➤ Who Do You Trust? (1957-63)

Kitchen Inventions

The 20th-century kitchen was a playground for food scientists and engineers with new labor-saving devices and culinary shortcuts launched every year. These all made their debut before you were 18.

1942	Vlasic pickles
1943	Uncle Ben's rice
1944	Dish drying cabinet
1945	Minute Maid orange concentrate
1946	Food processor
1946	Tupperware products
1947	Zen Rex speed peeler
1948	Aluminum foil
1949	**Reddi-Wip cream**

Reddi-Wip has been chosen as one of The Top 100 consumer inventions of 20th century and made its inventor, Aaron Lapin, the 'Whipped Cream King', millions of dollars.

1950	Green Garbage Bags
1951	Kenwood food mixer
1952	Automatic coffee pot
1952	Bread clip
1953	Combination washer-dryer
1954	Zipper storage bag
1955	Lint roller
1956	Saran wrap
1957	Homemaker tableware
1958	Rice-a-Roni
1959	Chocolate Velvet Cake invented

Around the World When You Turned 18

These are the headlines from around the globe as you were catapulted into adulthood.

- OPEC is founded
- Ban the Bomb rallies begin in UK
- Israel abducts Eichmann for war crimes
- Soviets shoot down spy plane
- Cameroon becomes independent
- Olympics open in Rome
- Aswan Dam begins construction
- Explorers descend into the Mariana Trench
- Cuba nationalizes all production and industry
- Large number of people flee East Berlin
- Sharpeville massacre takes place
- Niger becomes independent
- CERN particle accelerator operational
- The Beatles play Hamburg
- Berlin Wall construction begins
- Irish Republican Army starts attacking British forces
- Togo gains independence
- France tests the atomic bomb
- Tidal wave kills 12,000 in Morocco
- European Free Trade Association (EFTA) is established
- South Africa mine collapse kills 435
- Brasilia becomes Brazil's capital
- Powerful earthquake hits Chile
- Woman becomes prime minister of a country (Sri Lanka)
- Insurrection in Algiers opposing French rule

Super Bowl Champions Since You Were Born

These are the teams that have held a 7-pound, sterling silver Vince Lombardi trophy aloft during the Super Bowl era, and the number of times they've done it in your lifetime.

- **New England Patriots (6)**
  2001: The Super Bowl MVP, Tom Brady, had been a 6th round draft pick in 2000.

- Pittsburgh Steelers (6)
- Dallas Cowboys (5)
- San Francisco 49ers (5)
- **Green Bay Packers (4)**
  1967: To gain a berth in the Super Bowl, the Packers defeated the Dallas Cowboys in The Ice Bowl at 15 degrees below zero.

- New York Giants (4)
- **Denver Broncos (3)**
  2015: After the Broncos won their first Super Bowl 18 years prior, Broncos owner Pat Bowlen dedicated the victory to long-time quarterback John Elway ("This one's for John!"). After the 2015 victory, John Elway (now general manager) dedicated it to the ailing Bowlen ("This one's for Pat!").

- Washington Football Team (3)
- Las Vegas Raiders (3)
- Miami Dolphins (2)
- Indianapolis Colts (2)
- Kansas City Chiefs (2)
- Baltimore Ravens (2)
- Tampa Bay Buccaneers (2)
- **St. Louis/Los Angeles Rams (2)**
  1999: The Rams were led to the Super Bowl by Kurt Warner, who had been a grocery store clerk after college.

- Seattle Seahawks (1)
- Philadelphia Eagles (1)
- **Chicago Bears (1)**
  The 1985 Bears are known for their song, The Super Bowl Shuffle.

- New York Jets (1)
- New Orleans Saints (1)

Across the Nation

Voting. Joining the military. Turning 18 is serious stuff. Here's what everyone was reading about in the year you reached this milestone.

+ Birth control pill approved
+ Lucille Ball divorces Desi Arnaz
+ John F. Kennedy elected president (right)
+ USAF captain sets three parachute records from 100,000 feet
+ Arnold Palmer wins US Open
+ Actress Joanne Woodward given first Hollywood star
+ Laser patented—and 30-year dispute begins
+ Domino's Pizza opens in Michigan
+ Woolworth's lunch counter sit-in occurs
+ Civil Rights Acts of 1960 signed
+ Wilt Chamberlain sets record as 7'1" rookie in NBA
+ Wilma Rudolph wins three gold medals in 1960 Olympics
+ Cassius Clay "floats like a butterfly" to become heavyweight champ
+ Aluminum cans first used, for frozen juice
+ U-2 pilot captured by Soviet Union
+ New Orleans desegregation crisis begins
+ Pioneer 5 launched to map interplanetary magnetic field
+ Supreme Court decides Boynton v. Virginia
+ Nuclear-powered USS Enterprise launched
+ Winter Olympics hosted in California
+ Etch A Sketch goes on sale
+ The Twist becomes dance craze
+ US Hockey team wins gold medal
+ Pittsburgh Pirates win the World Series

Born this year:
∞ Apple CEO Tim Cook
∞ Actor Sean Penn
∞ John F. Kennedy Jr.

US Open Champions

Winners while you were between the ages of the youngest (John McDermott, 1911, 19 years) and the oldest (Hale Irwin, 1990, at 45). Planning a win? Better hurry up!

1961	Gene Littler
1962	Jack Nicklaus
1963	Julius Boros
1964	Ken Venturi
1965	**Gary Player** First non-US winner of the US Open since 1925.
1966	Billy Casper
1967	Jack Nicklaus
1968	Lee Trevino
1969	Orville Moody
1970	Tony Jacklin
1971	Lee Trevino
1972	Jack Nicklaus
1973	**Johnny Miller** In 1973, 61-year-old Sam Snead became the oldest player ever to make the cut.
1974	Hale Irwin
1975	Lou Graham
1976	Jerry Pate
1977	Hubert Green
1978	Andy North
1979	Hale Irwin
1980	**Jack Nicklaus** Nicklaus set the record for years (18) between the first and last US Open victory.
1981	David Graham
1982	Tom Watson
1983	Larry Nelson
1984	Fuzzy Zoeller
1985	Andy North
1986	Raymond Floyd
1987	Scott Simpson

Popular Girls' Names

If you started a family at a young age, these are the names you're most likely to have chosen. And even if you didn't pick them, a lot of Americans did!

Lisa
Lisa finally toppled Mary to take the top spot—and she'd stay there until 1969 (when she was usurped by Jennifer).

Mary
Susan
Karen
Linda
Patricia
Donna
Cynthia
Deborah
Sandra
Lori
Brenda
Pamela
Barbara
Debra
Kimberly
Sharon
Teresa
Nancy
Elizabeth
Laura
Julie
Tammy
Cheryl
Robin
Diane

Rising and falling stars:
Sherri, Penny and Andrea graced the Top 100 for the first time; for Peggy and Betty it would be their last ever year in the spotlight.

Animals Extinct in Your Lifetime

Billions of passenger pigeons once flew the US skies. By 1914, they had been trapped to extinction. Not every species dies at our hands, but it's a sobering roll-call. (Date is year last known alive or declared extinct).

1943	Desert bandicoot
1945	Wake Island rail
1949	Sinu parakeet
1951	Yemen gazelle
1952	**Deepwater cisco fish** The deepwater cisco, once found in Lake Huron and Michigan, was overfished and crowded out by invasive parasites and alewife herring. Result? Extinction.
1952	San Benedicto rock wren
1960	Candango mouse, Brasilia
1962	Red-bellied opossum, Argentina
1963	Kākāwahie honeycreeper, Hawaii
1964	South Island snipe, New Zealand
1966	Arabian ostrich
1967	Saint Helena earwig
1967	**Yellow blossom pearly mussel** Habitat loss and pollution proved terminal for this Tennessee resident.
1971	Lake Pedder earthworm, Tasmania
1972	Bushwren, New Zealand
1981	Southern gastric-brooding frog, Australia
1986	Las Vegas dace
1989	Golden toad (see right)
1990	Dusky seaside sparrow, East Coast USA
2000	**Pyrenean ibex, Iberia** For a few minutes in 2003 this species was brought back to life through cloning, but sadly the newborn female ibex died.
2001	Caspian tiger, Central Asia
2012	**Pinta giant tortoise** The rarest creature in the world for the latter half of his 100-year life, Lonesome George of the Galapagos was the last remaining Pinta tortoise.

The observed history of the golden toad is brief and tragic. It wasn't discovered until 1964, abundant in a pristine area of Costa Rica. By 1989 it had gone, a victim of rising temperatures.

Popular Boys' Names

Here are the top boys' names for this year. Many of the most popular choices haven't shifted much since you were born, but more modern names are creeping in…

Michael
For 44 years from 1954 onwards, Michael was the nation's most popular name. (There was one blip in 1960 when David came first.)

David
John
James
Robert
Mark
William
Richard
Thomas
Jeffrey
Scott
Steven
Joseph
Kevin
Charles
Timothy
Daniel
Kenneth
Paul
Brian
Gregory
Gary
Donald
Anthony
Ronald
Christopher
Douglas

Rising and falling stars:
Tom and Ronnie made their last appearance, while Jonathan made his first. Gregory peaked this year, in 21st place.

Popular Movies When You Were 21

The biggest stars in the biggest movies: these are the films the nation were enjoying as you entered into adulthood.

Son of Flubber 🎬 Fred MacMurray, Nancy Olson, Keenan Wynn

The Birds 🎬 Rod Taylor, Tippi Hedren, Jessica Tandy

It Happened at the World's Fair 🎬 Elvis Presley, Joan O'Brien, Gary Lockwood

Bye Bye Birdie 🎬 Janet Leigh, Dick Van Dyke, Ann-Margret
Elvis Presley was first choice for the role of Birdie but was overruled by Colonel Tom Parker.

Dr. No 🎬 Sean Connery, Ursula Andress, Joseph Wiseman

55 Days at Peking 🎬 Charlton Heston, Ava Gardner, David Niven

Hud 🎬 Paul Newman, Melvyn Douglas, Patricia Neal

Come Blow Your Horn 🎬 Frank Sinatra, Lee J. Cobb, Molly Picon

Cleopatra 🎬 Elizabeth Taylor, Richard Burton, Rex Harrison
Taylor set a Guinness World Record with 65 costume changes in a film.

Donovan's Reef 🎬 Lee Marvin, John Wayne, Jack Warden

Irma La Douce 🎬 Jack Lemmon, Shirley MacLaine, Lou Jacobi

Blood Feast 🎬 Mal Arnold William Kerwin, Connie Mason

The Thrill of it All 🎬 Doris Day, James Garner, Arlene Francis

The Great Escape 🎬 Steve McQueen, James Garner, Richard Attenborough

The V.I.P.s 🎬 Orson Welles, Margaret Rutherford, Elizabeth Taylor

Tom Jones 🎬 Albert Finney, Susannah York, Hugh Griffith

It's a Mad Mad Mad Mad World 🎬 Spencer Tracy, Milton Berle, Sid Caesar

McLintock! 🎬 John Wayne, Maureen O'Hara, Patrick Wayne

Fun in Acapulco 🎬 Elvis Presley, Ursula Andress, Paul Lukas

Charade 🎬 Cary Grant, Audrey Hepburn, Walter Matthau

The Cardinal 🎬 Tom Tryon, Romy Schneider, Carol Lynley

Move Over, Darling 🎬 Doris Day, James Garner, Polly Bergen

The Haunting 🎬 Julie Harris, Claire Bloom, Richard Johnson

Across the Nation

A selection of national headlines from the year you turned 21. But how many can you remember?

- ✦ Supreme Court decides Abington School District v. Schempp
- ✦ Minimum wage raised to $1.25
- ✦ Jack Nicklaus wins Masters golf tournament
- ✦ John F. Kennedy assassinated (right)
- ✦ Kids wish they were hotdogs (and sing on for the next 47 years)
- ✦ Kodak offers the Instamatic Camera
- ✦ Martin Luther King delivers "I Have a Dream" speech
- ✦ Zone Improvement Plan implemented by US Postal Service
- ✦ Lung successfully transplanted
- ✦ Prison on Alcatraz closes
- ✦ Partial Nuclear Test Ban Treaty approved
- ✦ Gideon v. Wainwright decided: no fair trial without counsel
- ✦ Four girls killed by bomb at Birmingham church
- ✦ "Hot line" between US and Soviet Union created
- ✦ Patsy Cline killed in plane crash
- ✦ First black graduate from University of Mississippi
- ✦ Touch tone phones introduced
- ✦ Pull tabs on soda cans patented
- ✦ Audio cassette released
- ✦ Valium becomes available
- ✦ Commercial nuclear power plant goes online
- ✦ Assassin Lee Harvey Oswald killed live on TV
- ✦ Lyndon B. Johnson sworn as president

Born this year:
- ⚭ Basketball legend Michael Jordan
- ⚭ Actor Brad Pitt
- ⚭ Singer Whitney Houston
- ⚭ Director Quentin Tarantino

Top: JFK chats to LBJ from his trademark rocking chair in September 1963. Three months on, JFK was assassinated. Within a day, all his possessions including the chair are removed from the White House. (The chair was given to JFK's brother-in-law and put up for auction in 2016.)

The Biggest Hits When You Were 21

The artists you love at 21 are with you for life. How many of these hits from this milestone year can you still hum or sing in the tub?

Inez and Charlie Foxx 🎤 Mockingbird
The Impressions 🎤 It's All Right
Roy Orbison 🎤 Blue Bayou
Johnny Cash 🎤 Ring of Fire
The Kingsmen 🎤 Louie Louie
Ruby and the Romantics 🎤 Our Day Will Come
Marty Robbins 🎤 Ruby Ann
Little Peggy March 🎤 I Will Follow Him
The Beatles 🎤 From Me to You
The Chiffons 🎤 He's So Fine
Leslie Gore 🎤 It's My Party
The Beach Boys 🎤 Surfin' USA
Bob Dylan 🎤 Blowin' in the Wind
Martha and the Vandellas 🎤 Heatwave
Steve Lawrence 🎤 Go Away Little Girl
Marvin Gaye 🎤 Can I Get a Witness
Bobby Vinton 🎤 Blue Velvet
The Drifters 🎤 Up on the Roof
Sam Cooke 🎤 Another Saturday Night
Allan Sherman 🎤 Hello Muddah, Hello Faddah
(A Letter from Camp)
Doris Troy 🎤 Just One Look
Bill Anderson 🎤 Still
Lester Flatt, Earl Scruggs
and the Foggy Mountain Boys 🎤 The Ballad of Jed Clampett
Dion and the Belmonts 🎤 Ruby Baby

Popular Food in the 1960s

Changes in society didn't stop at the front door: a revolution in the kitchen brought us exotic new recipes, convenience in a can, and even space-age fruit flavors. These are the tastes of a decade, but how many of them were on the menu for your family?

McDonald's Big Mac
First served in 1967 by a Pittsburgh franchisee.
Royal Shake-a-Pudd'n Dessert Mix
Tunnel of Fudge Cake
Campbell's SpaghettiOs
Pop-Tarts
B&M's canned bread
Cool Whip
A time-saving delight that originally contained no milk or cream, meaning that it could be frozen and transported easily.

Grasshopper pie
Beech-Nut Fruit Stripe Gum
Sandwich Loaf
Lipton Onion Soup Dip
Millions of packets are still sold each year of this favorite that was once known as "Californian Dip".

Jello salad
Hires Root Beer
Baked Alaska
Tang
Invented by William A. Mitchell who also concocted Cool Whip, Tang was used by astronauts to flavor the otherwise unpalatable water on board the Gemini and Apollo missions.

Corn Diggers
Teem soda
Eggo Waffles
Kraft Shake 'N Bake
Maypo oatmeal
In 1985, Dire Straights sang, "I want my MTV"—an echo of the stars who'd shouted the same words to promote the new station. But 30 years before that (and the inspiration for MTV's campaign), an animated child yelled, "I want my Maypo!"

Fashion in the Sixties

As a child, you (generally) wear what you're given. It's only in hindsight, on fading Polaroids, that you recognize that your outfits carried the fashion imprint of the day. Whether you were old or bold enough to carry off a pair of bell bottoms, though, is a secret that should remain between you and your photo albums.

Bell bottoms

Bell bottoms were widely available at Navy surplus and thrift stores at a time when second-hand shopping was on the rise.

Miniskirts and mini dresses

Peasant blouses

Rudi Gernreich

Pope Paul IV banned Catholics from wearing his monokini— a topless swim suit.

US flag clothing

Tulle turbans

Shift dresses

Collarless jackets

This jacket trend was popularized by the Beatles in 1963.

Babydoll dresses

V-neck tennis sweaters

Afghan coats

Leopard print clothing

In 1962, Jackie Kennedy wore a leopard print coat which caused a spike in demand for leopard skin, leading to the death of up to 250,000 leopards. The coat's designer, Oleg Cassini, felt guilty about it for the rest of his life.

Tie-dye clothing

Short, brightly colored, shapeless dresses

Pillbox hats

Mary Quant

Maxi skirts

Bonnie Cashin

Plaid

Poor boy sweaters

Pea coats

Around the World When You Turned 25

With the growing reach of news organizations, events from outside our borders were sometimes front-page news. How many do you remember?

- UK launches Ariel-3 satellite
- Heart transplant surgery is performed
- UK bans pirate radio stations
- Concorde is revealed
- Oil tanker accident causes ecological disaster in English Channel
- Che Guevara is captured
- People of Gibraltar vote to remain with UK
- Ocean liner is named for Elizabeth II
- British businessman completes solo sail around the world
- Sweden now drives on right
- Biafra declares independence from Nigeria
- UK and Ireland apply for EEC membership
- Soccer riot in Turkey kills 41
- EEC becomes European Community (EC)
- London bank installs ATM
- Leakey announces find in Kenya
- New Zealand adopts dollar
- Outer Space Treaty is signed
- Brushfires engulf southern Tasmania
- Stalin's daughter defects to the West
- Israel wins Six Day War against Arab nations
- Montreal hosts Expo 67
- Coup in Greece overthrows government
- Typhoon Emma strikes the Philippines
- China tests hydrogen bomb

rs of the 1960s

Smaller cars. More powerful cars. More distinctive cars. More variety, yes: but the success of imported models such as the Volkswagen Beetle was a sign that more fundamental changes lay ahead for The Big Three.

1940	Ford Lincoln Continental
1949	Volkswagen Beetle
1950	Volkswagen Type 2 (Microbus)
1958	**General Motors Chevrolet Impala** In 1965, the Impala sold more than 1 million units, the most sold by any model in the US since WWII.
1958	American Motors Corporation Rambler Ambassador
1959	General Motors Chevrolet El Camino
1959	Ford Galaxie
1960	**Ford Falcon** The cartoon strip "Peanuts" was animated for TV to market the Falcon.
1960	General Motors Pontiac Tempest
1960	General Motors Chevrolet Corvair
1961	**Jaguar E-Type** Ranked first in The Daily Telegraph UK's list of the world's "100 most beautiful cars" of all time.
1961	Chrysler Newport
1962	Shelby Cobra
1963	General Motors Buick Riviera
1963	Porsche 911
1963	Kaiser-Jeep Jeep Wagoneer
1964	**Ford Mustang** The song of the same name reached #6 on the R&B Charts in 1966. That year, more Ford Mustangs were sold (550,000) than any other car.
1964	General Motors Chevrolet Chevelle
1964	Chrysler Plymouth Barracuda
1964	General Motors Pontiac GTO
1967	General Motors Chevrolet Camaro
1967	Ford Mercury Cougar
1968	Chrysler Plymouth Road Runner

Books of the Decade

Were you a voracious bookworm in your twenties? Or a more reluctant reader, only drawn by the biggest titles of the day? Here are the new titles that fought for your attention.

1962	One Flew Over the Cuckoo's Nest by Ken Kesey
1962	Franny and Zooey by J.D. Salinger
1963	The Bell Jar by Sylvia Plath
1963	The Feminine Mystique by Betty Friedan
1963	A Clockwork Orange by Anthony Burgess
1964	The Group by Mary McCarthy
1964	Herzog by Saul Bellow
1964	The Spy Who Came in from the Cold by John le Carré
1964	Up the Down Staircase by Bel Kaufman
1965	Dune by Frank Herbert
1966	Valley of the Dolls by Jacqueline Susann
1966	In Cold Blood by Truman Capote
1967	Rosemary's Baby by Ira Levin
1967	The Arrangement by Elia Kazan
1967	The Confessions of Nat Turner by William Styron
1968	Airport by Arthur Hailey
1968	Couples by John Updike
1969	The Godfather by Mario Puzo
1969	Slaughterhouse-Five by Kurt Vonnegut
1969	Portnoy's Complaint by Philip Roth
1969	The French Lieutenant's Woman by John Fowles
1970	Love Story by Erich Segal
1970	One Hundred Years of Solitude by Gabriel Garcia Marquez
1971	The Happy Hooker: My Own Story by Xaviera Hollander
1971	The Exorcist by William Peter Blatty

Prominent Americans

This new set of definitive stamps, issued from 1965 onwards, aimed to do a better job of capturing the diversity of the Americans who made a nation. The series doubled the previous number of women depicted…to two. How many did you have in your collection?

Thomas Jefferson 1 ¢ 🖾 Third US President
Albert Gallatin 1 ¼ ¢ 🖾 Fourth Treasury Secretary
Frank Lloyd Wright 2 ¢ 🖾 Architect
Francis Parkman 3 ¢ 🖾 Historian
Abraham Lincoln 4 ¢ 🖾 16th US President
George Washington 5 ¢ 🖾 First US President
Franklin D Roosevelt 6 ¢ 🖾 32nd US President
Dwight Eisenhower 6 / 8 ¢ 🖾 34th US President
In 1957, Eisenhower became the first president to travel by helicopter instead of a limo, en route to Camp David (which he had called Shangri-La, but renamed after his grandson).

Benjamin Franklin 7 ¢ 🖾 Polymath
Albert Einstein 8 ¢ 🖾 Physicist
Andrew Jackson 10 ¢ 🖾 7th US President
Henry Ford 12 ¢ 🖾 Founder of Ford Motor Company
John F. Kennedy 13 ¢ 🖾 35th US President
Fiorello LaGuardia 14 ¢ 🖾 Mayor of New York City in WWII
Read Dick Tracy comics on the radio during a paper strike.

Oliver Wendell Holmes, Jr 15 ¢ 🖾 Supreme Court Justice
Ernie Pyle 16 ¢ 🖾 Journalist during World War II
Elizabeth Blackwell 18 ¢ 🖾 First woman to get a medical degree.
After 11 college rejections, male students at Geneva Medical College all voted for her acceptance. They did it as a joke.

George C Marshall 20 ¢ 🖾 Sec. of State and Sec. of Defense
Amadeo Giannini 21 ¢ 🖾 Founder of Bank of America
Frederick Douglass 25 ¢ 🖾 Slavery escapee, abolitionist leader
John Dewey 30 ¢ 🖾 Educational pioneer
Thomas Paine 40 ¢ 🖾 Helped inspire the American Revolution
Lucy Stone 50 ¢ 🖾 Suffragist and slavery campaigner
Eugene O'Neill $1 🖾 Playwright
John Bassett Moore $5 🖾 Jurist

Sixties Game Shows

Recovery from the quiz show scandal of the fifties was a gradual process. Big prize money was out; games were in—the sillier the better, or centered around relationships. "Popcorn for the mind," as game show creator Chuck Barris memorably put it.

College Bowl 🏆 (1953-70)
Snap Judgment 🏆 (1967-69)
To Tell The Truth 🏆 (1956-present)
Dough Re Mi 🏆 (1958-60)
Camouflage 🏆 (1961-62 & 1980)
Dream House 🏆 (1968-84)
Say When!! 🏆 (1961-65)
Let's Make A Deal 🏆 (1963-present)
The long-time presenter of the show, Monty Hall, gave rise to the eponymous problem: when one door in three hides a prize and you've made your pick, should you change your answer when the host reveals a "zonk" (dud) behind another door? (The counterintuitive answer is yes!)

Your First Impression 🏆 (1962-64)
Supermarket Sweep 🏆 (1965-present)
In one of its many comebacks, 1990 episodes of Supermarket Sweep featured monsters roaming the aisles including Frankenstein and Mr. Yuk.

You Don't Say! 🏆 1963-79)
It's Your Bet 🏆 (1969-73)
Yours For A Song 🏆 (1961-63)
Concentration 🏆 (1958-91)
Seven Keys 🏆 (1960-65)
Queen For A Day 🏆 1945-1970)
Password 🏆 (1961-75)
Video Village 🏆 (1960-62)
Who Do You Trust? 🏆 (1957-63)
Originally titled, "Do You Trust Your Wife?"
Personality 🏆 (1967-69)
Beat The Odds 🏆 (1961-69)

Across the Nation

Another decade passes and you're well into adulthood. Were you reading the news, or making it? Here are the national stories that dominated the front pages.

+ Nixon wins re-election
+ The world's greatest jewel heist? Eight rob the Pierre Hotel
+ Dallas Cowboys win the Super Bowl
+ Shirley Chisholm announces her run for president
+ Bob Douglas elected to Basketball Hall of Fame
+ Equal Rights Amendment passes
+ President Nixon visits China
+ Coal sludge spill kills over 125
+ Gov. George Wallace shot while campaigning for presidency
+ Watergate burglars arrested
+ Black Hills Flood strikes
+ Hurricane Agnes hits the East Coast
+ No new draftees to Vietnam announced
+ Supreme Court rules death penalty unconstitutional
+ Actress Jane Fonda tours Vietnam
+ Health officials admit to Tuskegee study scandal
+ Swimmer Mark Spitz wins 7 Olympic gold medals (right)
+ Riot breaks out on USS Kitty Hawk
+ FBI hires first female agents
+ HBO begins as subscription cable-provider service
+ Apollo 17 returns safely
+ Football's "Immaculate Reception" completed
+ Women run the Boston Marathon
+ Black Lung Benefit bill signed

Born this year:
- Rapper Eminem
- Actress Cameron Diaz
- Actor Ben Affleck

Seven events, seven gold medals, seven world records: Mark Spitz's performance at the 1972 Munich Olympics was unprecedented. It was another 36 years before his achievement was surpassed when Michael Phelps won 8 gold medals in Beijing.

The Biggest Hits When You Were 30...

How many of these big tunes from the year you turned thirty will still strike a chord decades later?

Don McLean 🎵 American Pie

Chicago 🎵 Saturday in the Park

3 Dog Night 🎵 Never Been to Spain

Neil Young 🎵 Heart of Gold

Harry Nilsson 🎵 Without You

Hot Butter 🎵 Popcorn

Bill Withers 🎵 Lean on Me

Jerry Lee Lewis 🎵 Chantilly Lace

Sammy Davis Jr. 🎵 The Candyman

Cat Stevens 🎵 Morning Has Broken

Looking Glass 🎵 Brandy (You're a Fine Girl)

John Fogerty
and the Blue Ridge Rangers 🎵 Jambalaya (On the Bayou)

Billy Paul 🎵 Me and Mrs. Jones

Donna Fargo 🎵 The Happiest Girl in the Whole USA

Stevie Wonder 🎵 Superstition

Elton John 🎵 Crocodile Rock

The Main Ingredient 🎵 Everybody Plays the Fool

Faron Young 🎵 It's Four in the Morning

The Moody Blues 🎵 Nights in White Satin

Harold Melvin
and the Blue Notes 🎵 If You Don't Know Me by Now

Roberta Flack 🎵 The First Time Ever I Saw Your Face

The Staple Singers 🎵 I'll Take You There

Gilbert O'Sullivan 🎵 Alone Again (Naturally)

Dr. Hook and
the Medicine Show 🎵 The Cover of the Rolling Stone

(30) ...and the Movies You Saw That Year, Too

From award winners to crowd pleasers, here are the movies that played as your third decade drew to a close.

Joe Kidd 🎬 Clint Eastwood, Robert Duvall, John Saxon

Lady Sings the Blues 🎬 Diana Ross, Billy Dee Williams, Richard Pryor

Sounder 🎬 Cicely Tyson, Paul Winfield, Kevin Hooks

The Last House on the Left 🎬 Sandra Peabody, Lucy Grantham, David A. Hess

Tokyo Story 🎬 Chishu Ryu, Chieko Higashiyama, Setsuko Hara

Shaft's Big Score 🎬 Richard Roundtree, Moses Gunn

Across 110th Street 🎬 Yaphet Kotto, Anthony Quinn, Anthony Franciosa
Anthony Quinn had wanted Sidney Poitier to play Lt. Pope.

The Valachi Papers 🎬 Charles Bronson, Lino Ventura, Jill Ireland

Last Tango in Paris 🎬 Marlon Brando, Maria Schneider, Maria Michi

Deep Throat 🎬 Linda Lovelace, Harry Reems, Dolly Sharp

The Life and Times of Judge Roy Bean 🎬 Paul Newman, Jacqueline Bisset, Anthony Perkins

Pete 'n' Tillie 🎬 Walter Matthau, Carol Burnett, Geraldine Page

Frenzy 🎬 Jon Finch, Alec McCowen, Barry Foster

Everything You Always Wanted to Know About Sex 🎬 Woody Allen, John Carradine, Lou Jacobi

The Cowboys 🎬 John Wayne, Roscoe Lee Browne, Slim Pickens

What's Up, Doc? 🎬 Barbra Streisand, Ryan O'Neal, Kenneth Mars

Cabaret 🎬 Liza Minnelli, Michael York, Joel Grey

Deliverance 🎬 Jon Voight, Ned Beatty, Ronny Cox

Banshun 🎬 Chishu Ryu, Setsuko Hara, Haruko Sugimura

The Godfather 🎬 Marlon Brando, Al Pacino, James Caan

Conquest of the Planet of the Apes 🎬 Roddy McDowall, Don Murray, Ricardo Montalban

The Poseidon Adventure 🎬 Gene Hackman, Ernest Borgnine, Red Buttons

The Getaway 🎬 Steve McQueen, Ali MacGraw, Ben Johnson

Jeremiah Johnson 🎬 Robert Redford, Will Geer, Allyn Ann McLerie

Around the House

Sometimes with a fanfare but often by stealth, inventions and innovations transformed the 20th-century household. Here's what arrived between the ages of 10 and 30.

1953	**WD-40 spray** Now a household essential, "Water Displacement 40th Formula" was created for the aerospace industry to protect, clean, and lubricate—much as it is now used by everyone else.
1955	TV remote control
1956	Snooze alarm clock
1956	Velcro
1957	Off mosquito repellent
1957	First electric watch
1958	Friskies cat food
1961	Head & Shoulders shampoo
1963	**Chips Ahoy! chocolate chip cookies** An elementary teacher and her class wrote Nabisco saying that they did not find 1000 chips in the bag of Chips Ahoy, though the bag clearly states it has that many. Nabisco flew a representative to their school and demonstrated to the students (and the media) how to actually find all the chips.
1963	Push button Touchtone phone
1963	Lava lamps
1964	Portable TVs
1964	Sharpie permanent markers
1965	Cordless telephone
1968	Bean bag chair
1969	Nerf dart guns
1970	**Irish Spring soap** Irish Spring soap's catchy tune and tag lines became part of the language with "Clean as a whistle" and "I like it too!" While it generated a lot of bad Irish accents, it has nothing to do with Ireland.
1971	Soft contact lenses

Here's one that didn't quite make the grade: AT&T's Picturephone, demonstrated here at the 1964 New York World's Fair. A trial set up that year invited the public to rent two of the Picturephone rooms set up in New York, Chicago, and Washington ($16 for 3 minutes). The take-up over the following years was almost nil, but Picturephones went on sale in 1970 anyway with a prediction of a billion-dollar business by 1980. The devices

Female Olympic Gold Medalists in Your Lifetime

These are the women who have stood atop the podium the greatest number of times at the Summer Olympics, whether in individual or team events.

Jenny Thompson (8) Swimming
Thompson is an anesthesiologist. She started her medical training in 2000—although she took time out while studying to win further gold World Championship medals.

Katie Ledecky (7) Swimming
Allyson Felix (7) Athletics
Amy Van Dyken (6) Swimming
Dana Vollmer (5) Swimming
Missy Franklin (5) Swimming
Sue Bird (5) Basketball
Diana Taurasi (5) Basketball
The late Kobe Bryant dubbed Taurasi the "white mamba"; for others she is the G.O.A.T. in women's basketball.

Allison Schmitt (4) Swimming
Dara Torres (4) Swimming
Evelyn Ashford (4) Athletics
Janet Evans (4) Swimming
Lisa Leslie (4) Basketball
Pat McCormick (4) Diving
Sanya Richards-Ross (4) Athletics
Serena Williams (4) Tennis
Simone Biles (4) Gymnastics
Biles's phenomenal medal tally in Olympics and World Championships is greater than any other US gymnast.

Tamika Catchings (4) Basketball
Teresa Edwards (4) Basketball
Venus Williams (4) Tennis

Around the World When You Turned 35

(35)

It's a big news day every day, somewhere in the world. Here are the stories that the media thought you'd want to read in the year of your 35th birthday.

+ Australia's worst rail accident kills 83 in Sydney
+ Anwar Sadat visits Israel
+ Panama gains control of Panama Canal
+ Indira Gandhi resigns as prime minister
+ Post-Franco Spain holds elections
+ Tenerife planes collide: 583 die in world's worst air disaster
+ Chaplin dies
+ Brazil's Pele retires from soccer
+ Public trade unions strike in UK
+ Race riots erupt in Bermuda
+ Bucharest is shaken by earthquake
+ Quebec adopts French as official language
+ Israel elects Begin as prime minister
+ Cyclone in India results in thousands dead and millions become homeless
+ Elizabeth II celebrates Jubilee (25 years of rule)
+ Terrorists set off three bombs in Moscow
+ Volcano erupts in Zaire
+ Last execution by guillotine in France
+ Blizzard causes houses to collapse in Northern Japan
+ War begins between Vietnam and Cambodia
+ Dutch school taken over by terrorists
+ Virginia Wade wins Wimbledon
+ Libya and Egypt go to war
+ Japan's Mount Usu erupts
+ Last natural smallpox case discovered

Drinks of the Sixties

For many of those slipping from adolescence into adulthood, your choice of drink says a lot about you. Sophisticated or down-to-earth? A classic, or something to make a statement? In the years that follow, the drinks might change, but the decision remains the same! Here's what was behind a sixties bar.

Falstaff beer
Rusty Nail cocktail
Rumored to be a favorite drink of the Rat Pack.

Hull's Cream Ale
Stinger cocktail
Rheingold Extra Dry Lager
Gunther's Beer
Lone Star Beer
The Gimlet cocktail
The Grasshopper cocktail
Little King's Cream Ale
Best known for its miniature seven-ounce bottles.

Mai Thai cocktail
Genesee Cream Ale
Storz Beer
From Nebraska, Storz was "Brewed for the beer pro."

Iron City Beer
Iron City is reputed to have introduced the first twist-off bottle cap in 1963.

Golden Dream cocktail
Mint Julep cocktail
It's the official drink of the Kentucky Derby, with around 120,000 served over the weekend.

Koch's Light Lager Beer
Arrow 77 Beer
Daiquiri cocktail
Manhattan cocktail
Sterling Premium Pilsner
Carling Black Label
Hamm's Beer
Old fashioned cocktail

Seventies Game Shows

With enough water under the bridge since the 1950s scandals, producers of seventies game shows injected big money into new formats and revamped favorites, some of them screened five nights a week. How many did you cheer on from the couch?

High Rollers 🏆 (1974-88)

Gambit 🏆 (1972-81)

The New Treasure Hunt 🏆 (1973-82)
Perhaps the best-known episode of this show saw a woman faint when she won a Rolls Royce—that she later had to sell in order to pay the taxes.

The Cross-Wits 🏆 (1975-87)

Hollywood Squares 🏆 1966-2004)

The Newlywed Game 🏆 (1966-2013)
Show creator Chuck Barris also made "3's a Crowd"— the show in which men, their secretaries and their wives competed. The public wasn't happy.

Pyramid 🏆 (1973-present)
Thanks to inflation and rival prizes, the $10,000 Pyramid in 1973 didn't last long: from 1976 it was raised in increments to its current peak of $100,000.

Dealer's Choice 🏆 (1974-75)

Sports Challenge 🏆 (1971-79)

Tattletales 🏆 (1974-84)

It's Your Bet 🏆 (1969-73)

Celebrity Sweepstakes 🏆 (1974-77)

Rhyme and Reason 🏆 (1975-76)

Three On A Match 🏆 (1971-74)

The Match Game 🏆 (1962-present)

Sale of the Century 🏆 (1969-89)

The Dating Game 🏆 (1965-99)
The Dating Game—known as Blind Date in many international versions—saw many celebrity appearances before they became well-known, including the Carpenters and Arnold Schwarzenegger.

Popular Boys' Names

Just as middle age crept up unnoticed, so the most popular names also evolved. The traditional choices—possibly including yours—are fast losing their appeal to new parents.

Michael

Christopher

Matthew

For fourteen years from 1980, tastes in baby names were locked tight at the top: Michael was the most popular, Christopher was runner-up with Matthew in third spot.

Jason

David

James

Joshua

John

Robert

Daniel

Joseph

Justin

Ryan

Brian

William

Jonathan

Andrew

Brandon

Adam

Eric

Nicholas

Anthony

Thomas

Kevin

Timothy

Steven

Rising and falling stars:

Debutants in 1982: Ian, Jordan and Cody. Off into the sunset go Shaun, Russell and Jerry.

Popular Girls' Names

40

It's a similar story for girls' names. Increasing numbers are taking their infant inspiration from popular culture. The worlds of music, film and theater are all fertile hunting grounds for those in need of inspiration.

Jennifer
Jessica
Amanda
Sarah
Melissa
Nicole
Stephanie
Elizabeth

A name's moment in the sun spans years, sometimes decades. But eventually they disappear out of sight... unless you're Elizabeth. For over a century she's floated between 6th and 26th position.

Crystal
Amy
Michelle
Heather
Tiffany
Kimberly
Rebecca
Angela
Ashley
Amber
Christina
Erin
Rachel
Laura
Lisa
Emily
Kelly

Rising and falling stars:

Girls we welcomed for the first time this year: Cassandra, Krystal, Alexis, Brittany, Jillian and Nichole. Names we'd never see in the Top 100 again: Dawn, Lori and Denise.

NBA Champions Since You Were Born

These are the winners of the NBA Finals in your lifetime—and the number of times they've taken the title.

- Philadelphia Warriors (2)
- Baltimore Bullets (1)
- Minneapolis Lakers (5)
- Rochester Royals (1)
- Syracuse Nationals (1)
- **Boston Celtics (17)**
  1966: After the Lakers won Game 1 of the NBA Finals, the Celtics named their star Bill Russell player-coach. He was the first black coach in the NBA. The Celtics responded by winning the series.

- St. Louis Hawks (1)
- Philadelphia 76ers (2)
- New York Knicks (2)
- Milwaukee Bucks (2)
- **Los Angeles Lakers (12)**
  1980: With Kareem Abdul-Jabbar out with an injury, Lakers' 20-year-old rookie Magic Johnson started at center in the clinching Game 6 and scored 42 points and snared 15 rebounds.

- **Golden State Warriors (4)**
  2015: LeBron James and Stephen Curry, the stars of the teams that faced off in the 2015 NBA Finals, were both born in the same hospital in Akron, Ohio.

- Portland Trail Blazers (1)
- Washington Bullets (1)
- Seattle SuperSonics (1)
- Detroit Pistons (3)
- Chicago Bulls (6)
- Houston Rockets (2)
- San Antonio Spurs (5)
- Miami Heat (3)
- Dallas Mavericks (1)
- Cleveland Cavaliers (1)
- Toronto Raptors (1)

Fashion in the Seventies

The decade that taste forgot? Or a kickback against the sixties and an explosion of individuality? Skirts got shorter (and longer). Block colors and peasant chic vied with sequins and disco glamor. How many of your seventies outfits would you still wear today?

Wrap dresses
Diane von Fürstenberg said she invented the silent, no-zipper wrap dress for one-night stands. "Haven't you ever tried to creep out of the room unnoticed the following morning? I've done that many times."

Tube tops
Midi skirt
In 1970, fashion designers began to lower the hemlines on the mini skirt. This change wasn't welcomed by many consumers. Women picketed in New York City with "stop the midi" signs.

Track suit, running shoes, soccer jerseys
Cowl neck sweaters
His & hers matching outfits
Cork-soled platform shoes
Caftans, Kaftans, Kimonos and mummus
Prairie dresses
Cuban heels
Gaucho pants
Chokers and dog collars as necklaces
Birkenstocks
Tennis headbands
Turtleneck shirts
Puffer vests
Long knit vests layered over tops and pants
Military surplus rucksack bags
"Daisy Dukes" denim shorts
Daisy's revealing cut-off denim shorts in The Dukes of Hazzard caught the attention of network censors. The answer for actor Catherine Bach? Wear flesh-colored pantyhose—just in case.

Yves Saint Laurent
Shrink tops
Bill Gibb

Drinks of the Seventies

Breweries were bigger, and there were fewer of them. Beers were lighter. But what could you (or your parents) serve with your seventies fondue? How about a cocktail that's as heavy on the double-entendre as it was on the sloe gin? Or perhaps match the decade's disco theme with a splash of blue curaçao?

Amber Moon cocktail
Features an unbroken, raw egg and featured in the film Murder on the Orient Express.

Billy Beer
Rainier Beer
Point Special Lager
Tequila Sunrise cocktail
Regal Select Light Beer
Stroh's rum
Long Island Iced Tea cocktail
Merry Widow cocktail
Shell's City Pilsner Premium Beer
Brass Monkey cocktail
The Godfather cocktail
Brown Derby
Sea-Breeze cocktail

Schlitz
This Milwaukee brewery was the country's largest in the late sixties and early seventies. But production problems were followed by a disastrous ad campaign, and by 1981 the original brewery was closed.

Alabama Slammer cocktail
Golden Cadillac cocktail
Harvey Wallbanger cocktail
Red White & Blue Special Lager Beer
Lite Beer from Miller

Coors Banquet Beer
A beer that made the most of its initial limited distribution network by floating the idea of contraband Coors. The idea was so successful that Coors smuggling became central to the plot of the movie Smokey and the Bandit.

US Open Tennis

Across the Open Era and the US National Championship that preceded it, these men won between the year you turned 19 (matching the youngest ever champ, Pete Sampras) and 38 (William Larned's age with his seventh win, in 1911).

1961	Roy Emerson
1962	Rod Laver
1963	Rafael Osuna
1964	Roy Emerson
1965	Manuel Santana
1966	Fred Stolle
1967	**John Newcombe**

Newcombe was George W. Bush's drinking companion the day in 1976 when Bush was charged with driving under the influence of alcohol.

1968	Arthur Ashe
1969	Rod Laver
1970	Ken Rosewall
1971	Stan Smith
1972	Illie Nastase
1973	John Newcombe
1974	Jimmy Connors
1975	**Manuel Orantes**

Orantes came back from 5-0 down in the 4th set of the semifinal to win the 4th and 5th sets and upset top-seeded Jimmy Connors in the final.

1976	Jimmy Connors
1977	Guillermo Vilas
1978	**Jimmy Connors**

Connors became the only player to win on all three surfaces that have been used by the US Open.

1979-81	John McEnroe

Books of the Decade

Family, friends, TV, and more: there are as many midlife distractions as there are books on the shelf. Did you get drawn in by these bestsellers, all published in your thirties?

1972	Watership Down by Richard Adams
1972	The Joy of Sex by Alex Comfort
1972	Fear and Loathing in Las Vegas by Hunter S. Thompson
1973	Fear of Flying by Erica Jong
1973	Gravity's Rainbow by Thomas Pynchon
1974	Jaws by Peter Benchley
1974	The Front Runner by Patricia Nell Warren
1975	The Eagle Has Landed by Jack Higgins
1975	Shōgun by James Clavell
1975	Ragtime by E.L. Doctorow
1976	Roots by Alex Haley
1976	The Hite Report by Shere Hite
1977	The Thorn Birds by Colleen McCullough
1977	The Women's Room by Marilyn French
1978	Eye of the Needle by Ken Follett
1978	The World According to Garp by John Irving
1979	Flowers in the Attic by V.C. Andrews
1979	The Hitchhiker's Guide to the Galaxy by Douglas Adams
1979	Sophie's Choice by William Styron
1980	Rage of Angels by Sidney Sheldon
1980	The Bourne Identity by Robert Ludlum
1980	The Covenant by James Michener
1981	The Hotel New Hampshire by John Irving
1981	Noble House by James Clavell
1981	An Indecent Obsession by Colleen McCullough

Around the World When You Turned 40

(40)

International stories from farflung places—but did they appear on your radar as you clocked up four decades on the planet?

- Canada signs Proclamation of the Constitution Act
- UK defeats Argentina over the Falklands
- Carlos the Jackal increases terror attacks in France
- Lebanese militia murder Palestinian refugees
- Israel returns Sinai to Egypt
- IRA bombs explode in London
- Man breaks into Queen Elizabeth's bedroom
- International Whaling Commission ends commercial whaling
- Arafat is elected as president of Palestine National Council
- World's largest oil rig sinks in North Atlantic
- Italy wins the World Cup
- Brezhnev dies
- Thousands die in Mexico after earthquake and volcano eruption
- Pope visits Great Britain
- Spanish priest tries to kill Pope John Paul II
- Israel declares war on Lebanon
- Mudslides kill hundreds in Nagasaki
- Princess Grace of Monaco dies
- Several die in crowd crush at a Moscow arena
- Italy wins Spain World Cup
- UN declares International Day of Peace
- Tanker explosion in Afghanistan kills over 150 people
- Lech Walesa released from internment in Poland
- Protesters are murdered in Suriname
- Bijon Setu massacre occurs in India

Across the Nation

Here are the headline stories from across the country in the year you hit 40.

- FedEx "Fast Talker" ads air
- AT&T ordered to break up as a monopoly
- Dozens of cities hit record low temperatures
- USA Today begins publishing
- Over 10 million dollars in cash stolen from armored car
- Disney's EPCOT Center opens
- Protestors gather against nuclear proliferation
- Tylenol laced with cyanide: seven die but nobody caught
- Successful permanent artificial heart implanted
- Vietnam War Memorial dedicated
- Emoticon smiley invented
- First application offered as freeware
- Grace Kelly dies in car crash
- Weather Channel begins broadcasting
- Commodore 64 goes on sale
- Actor John Belushi dies by overdose
- Air Florida Flight 90 crashes on takeoff into Potomac River (right)
- San Francisco 49ers win the Super Bowl
- St. Louis Cardinals win the World Series
- Jimmy Connors wins Wimbledon
- Man uses a lawn chair and weather balloons to fly above LA
- Actor Vic Morrow and two children killed in accident on movie set
- Rocker Ozzy Osbourne eats a bat onstage
- War on Drugs announced
- Chris Evert wins her 6th (and final) US Open title

Born this year:
- Singer Kelly Clarkson
- Actress Anne Hathaway
- Politician Pete Buttigieg

Navy divers search in the Potomac River after Air Florida Flight 90 crashed into the 14th Street Bridge on January 13. Only five of the 79 aboard survived, and four motorists on the bridge were killed. Passenger Arland Williams survived the crash but repeatedly passed lifelines to others in the water before drowning. An investigation found pilot error—the aircraft had not been properly de-iced and the plane couldn't gain enough altitude to clear the bridge.

The Biggest Hits When You Were 40

Big tunes for a big birthday: how many of them enticed your middle-aged party guests onto the dance floor?

Joan Jett and the Blackhearts 🎤 I Love Rock 'n' Roll

Culture Club 🎤 Do You Really Want to Hurt Me

Dexys Midnight Runners 🎤 Come on Eileen

Willie Nelson 🎤 Always on My Mind

Paul McCartney
and Stevie Wonder 🎤 Ebony and Ivory

The Human League 🎤 Don't You Want Me

Men at Work 🎤 Down Under

Dolly Parton 🎤 I Will Always Love You

Fleetwood Mac 🎤 Gypsy

Afrika Bambaataa 🎤 Planet Rock

Survivor 🎤 Eye of the Tiger

The Clash 🎤 Rock the Casbah

Alabama 🎤 Mountain Music

Billy Joel 🎤 She's Got a Way

Tommy Tutone 🎤 867-5309/Jenny

George Benson 🎤 Turn Your Love Around

The Go-Go's 🎤 Vacation

Merle Haggard 🎤 Are the Good Times Really Over
(I Wish a Buck Was Still Silver)

Musical Youth 🎤 Pass the Dutchie

George Thorogood
and the Destroyers 🎤 Bad to the Bone

Dazz Band 🎤 Let it Whip

Rush 🎤 New World Man

Stevie Wonder 🎤 That Girl

Toni Basil 🎤 Mickey

Popular Food in the 1970s

From fads to ads, here's a new collection of dinner party dishes and family favorites. This time it's the seventies that's serving up the delights—and some of us are still enjoying them today!

Watergate Salad
Black Forest cake
Chex Mix
Cheese Tid-Bits
Dolly Madison Koo-koos (cupcakes)
Life Cereal
"I'm not gonna try it. You try it. Let's get Mikey...he hates everything." Three on- and off-screen brothers, one memorable ad that ran for much of the seventies.

The Manwich
"A sandwich is a sandwich, but a manwich is a meal," the ads announced in 1969.

Tomato aspic
Bacardi rum cake
Impossible pies
Zucchini bread
Oscar Mayer bologna
Poke Cake made with Jell-O
Libbyland Dinners
Reggie! Bar
Named after New York Yankees' right fielder Reggie Jackson and launched as a novely, Reggie! Bars were on sale for six years.

Hostess Chocodiles
Polynesian chicken salad
Salmon mousse
Cheese log appetizer
Gray Poupon Dijon Mustard
Tootsie Pop
So how many licks does it take to get to the center of a Tootsie Pop? 364, and that's official: it was tested on a "licking machine."

..rs of the 1970s

A decade of strikes, federal regulations, foreign imports, oil crises, safety and quality concerns: car sales were up overall, but the US industry was under pressure like never before. Iconic new models to debut include the Pontiac Firebird and the outrageous, gold-plated Stutz Blackhawk.

1940	**Chrysler New Yorker**
	When is a New Yorker not a New Yorker? The eighth generation of this upscale car bore little resemblance to the 1940 launch models. Yet in 1970, the New Yorker was barely middle-aged: they lived on until 1997.
1948	Ford F-Series
1959	General Motors Cadillac Coupe de Ville
1959	Chrysler Plymouth Valiant
1960	Chrysler Dodge Dart
1961	**General Motors Oldsmobile Cutlass**
	The Cutlass outsold any other model in US for four consecutive years, notching up nearly 2 million sales.
1962	General Motors Chevrolet Nova
1965	General Motors Chevrolet Caprice
1965	Ford LTD
1967	General Motors Pontiac Firebird
1968	BMW 2002
1970	Chrysler Dodge Challenger
1970	General Motors Chevrolet Monte Carlo
1970	General Motors Chevrolet Vega
1970	American Motors Corporation Hornet
1970	Ford Maverick
1971	Nissan Datsun 240Z
1971	**Stutz Blackhawk**
	These luxury automobiles started at a cool $22,000 ($150,000 today); the first car sold went to Elvis. Among the many other celebrity Blackhawk owners was Dean Martin; one of his three models sported the vanity plate DRUNKY. He crashed it.
1971	Ford Pinto
1973	Honda Civic
1975	Ford Granada
1978	Ford Fiesta

US Banknotes

The cast of US banknotes hasn't changed in your lifetime, giving you plenty of time to get to know them. (Although if you have a lot of pictures of James Madison and Salmon P. Chase around the house, you might want to think about a visit to the bank.)

Fifty cent paper coin (1862–1876) 💵 Abraham Lincoln
These bills were known as "shinplasters" because the quality of the paper was so poor that they could be used to bandage leg wounds during the Civil War.

One dollar bill (1862–1869) 💵 Salmon P. Chase
The US Secretary of Treasury during Civil War, Salmon P. Chase is credited with putting the phrase "In God we trust" on US currency beginning in 1864.

One dollar bill (1869–present) 💵 George Washington
Some bills have a star at the end of the serial number. This means they are replacement bills for those printed with errors.

One silver dollar certificate (1886-96) 💵 Martha Washington
Two dollar bill (1862–present) 💵 Thomas Jefferson
Two dollar bills have a reputation of being rare, but there are actually 600 million in circulation in the US.

Five dollar bill (1914–present) 💵 Abraham Lincoln
Ten dollar bill (1914–1929) 💵 Andrew Jackson
Ten dollar bill (1929–present) 💵 Alexander Hamilton
Twenty dollar bill (1865–1869) 💵 Pocahontas
Twenty dollar bill (1914–1929) 💵 Grover Cleveland
Twenty dollar bill (1929–present) 💵 Andrew Jackson
Fifty dollar bill (1914–present) 💵 Ulysses S. Grant
One hundred dollar bill (1914–1929) 💵 Benjamin Franklin
The one hundred dollar bill has an expected circulation life of 22.9 years while the one dollar bill has an expected circulation life of just 6.6 years.

Five hundred dollar bill (1918–1928) 💵 John Marshall
Five hundred dollar bill (1945–1969) 💵 William McKinley
One thousand dollar bill (1918–1928) 💵 Alexander Hamilton
One thousand dollar bill (1928–1934) 💵 Grover Cleveland
Five thousand dollar bill (1918–1934) 💵 James Madison
Ten thousand dollar bill (1928–1934) 💵 Salmon P. Chase

Male Olympic Gold Medalists in Your Lifetime

These are the male athletes that have scooped the greatest number of individual and team gold medals at the Summer Olympics in your lifetime.

Michael Phelps (23) 🏅 Swimming (right)

Carl Lewis (9) 🏅 Athletics

Mark Spitz (9) 🏅 Swimming

For 36 years, Spitz's 7-gold-medal haul at the 1972 Munich Olympics was unbeaten; Michael Phelps finally broke the spell with his eighth gold in Beijing.

Matt Biondi (8) 🏅 Swimming

Caeleb Dressel (7) 🏅 Swimming

Ryan Lochte (6) 🏅 Swimming

Don Schollander (5) 🏅 Swimming

Gary Hall Jr. (5) 🏅 Swimming

Aaron Peirsol (5) 🏅 Swimming

Nathan Adrian (5) 🏅 Swimming

Tom Jager (5) 🏅 Swimming

Al Oerter Jr. (4) 🏅 Athletics

Four out of four: Oerter won Olympic gold medals in the discus in every Games from 1956-1968. He fought injuries that required him to wear a neck brace for the 1964 Tokyo Olympics—but he still set an Olympic record.

Greg Louganis (4) 🏅 Diving

Jason Lezak (4) 🏅 Swimming

John Naber (4) 🏅 Swimming

Jon Olsen (4) 🏅 Swimming

Lenny Krayzelburg (4) 🏅 Swimming

Matt Grevers (4) 🏅 Swimming

Michael Johnson (4) 🏅 Athletics

Once the fastest man in the world over 200 meters, Johnson took 15 minutes to walk the same distance in 2018 following a mini-stroke—but took it as a sign that he'd make a full recovery.

Harrison Dillard (4) 🏅 Athletics

Dillard—known as "Bones" for his skinny build—aspired to match the feats of his idol, Jesse Owens. And he did, becoming the only man to win gold as a sprinter and a hurdler.

Between 2000 and 2016, Michael Phelps won 28 Olympic medals, including 23 gold and 16 for individual events. That's 10 more than his nearest competitor, Larisa Latynina, a gymnast of the Soviet Union who took her last gold medal fifty years earlier.

Winter Olympics Venues Since You Were Born

Unless you're an athlete or winter sports fan, the Winter Olympics can slip past almost unnoticed. These are the venues; can you remember the host countries and years?

Lillehammer
Cortina d'Ampezzo
Oslo
Salt Lake City
Sapporo
Albertville
The last Games to be held in the same year as the Summer Olympics, with the next Winter Olympics held two years later.

Turin
Grenoble
Beijing
Sarajevo
Lake Placid
Sochi
Innsbruck (twice)
This usually snowy city experienced its mildest winter in 60 years; the army transported snow and ice from the mountains. Nevertheless, twelve years later, the Winter Olympics were back.

Squaw Valley
Nagano
St Moritz
The first Winter Olympics to be held for 12 years and named the 'Games of Renewal'; Japan and Germany were not invited.

Calgary
Vancouver
PyeongChang

Answers: *Lillehammer: Norway, 1994; Cortina d'Ampezzo: Italy, 1956; Oslo: Norway, 1952; Salt Lake City: USA, 2002; Sapporo: Japan, 1972; Albertville: France, 1992; Turin: Italy, 2006; Grenoble: France, 1968; Beijing: China, 2022; Sarajevo: Yugoslavia, 1984; Lake Placid: USA, 1980; Sochi: Russia, 2014; Innsbruck: Austria, 1964; Squaw Valley: USA, 1960; Nagano: Japan, 1998; St Moritz: Switzerland, 1948; Calgary: Canada, 1988; Innsbruck: Austria, 1976; Vancouver: Canada, 2010; PyeongChang: South Korea, 2018*

Fashion in the Eighties

Eighties fashion was many things, but subtle wasn't one of them. Influences were everywhere from aerobics to Wall Street, from pop princesses to preppy polo shirts. The result was chaotic, but fun. How many eighties throwbacks still lurk in your closet?

Stirrup pants

Ralph Lauren

Ruffled shirts

Jean Paul Gaultier

Acid wash jeans

Stone washing had been around a while, but the acid wash trend came about by chance—Rifle jeans of Italy accidentally tumbled jeans, bleach, and pumice stone with a little water. The result? A fashion craze was born.

Camp collar shirt with horizontal stripes

Thierry Mugler

Oversized denim jackets

Scrunchies

"Members Only" jackets

Members Only military-inspired jackets were marketed with the tagline "When you put it on...something happens."

Paper bag waist pants

Pleated stonewash baggy jeans

Cut-off sweatshirts/hoodies

Vivienne Westwood

Azzedine Alaia

Shoulder pads

Dookie chains

Leg warmers

Bally shoes

Jordache jeans

Calvin Klein

Windbreaker jackets

Ray-Ban Wayfarer sunglasses

Popularized by Tom Cruise in the movie Risky Business.

Parachute pants

Jumpsuits

World Buildings

Some of the most striking and significant buildings in the world sprang up when you were between 25 and 50 years old. How many do you know?

1967	Habitat 67
1968	Museum of Art of São Paulo Assis Chateaubriand
1970	Cathedral of Brasília
1971	Näsinneula tower, Tampere, Finland
1972	Olympiastadion, Munich
1973	**The Sydney Opera House** The iconic Sydney Opera House sits on the tip of Bennelong Point—on a site that previously homed a tram shed.
1975	First Canadian Place, Toronto
1976	The CN Tower, Toronto
1977	**The Centre Pompidou, Paris** The Centre Pompidou, known locally as Beaubourg, is considered the "inside-out" landmark—its structure and mechanical services are outside the building.
1978	Sunshine 60, Tokyo
1979	Kuwait Towers, Kuwait City
1980	Hopewell Centre, Hong Kong
1981	Sydney Tower
1982	First Canadian Centre, Calgary
1983	Teresa Carreño Cultural Complex, Caracus
1984	Deutsche Bank Twin Towers, Frankfurt
1985	Exchange Square, Hong Kong
1986	**Baha'i Lotus Temple, New Delhi** The Lotus Temple is open to all faiths to come worship, but no images, pictures, sermons, or even musical instruments are permitted.
1987	Fuji Xerox Towers, Singapore
1988	Canterra Tower, Calgary
1989	The Louvre Pyramid, Paris
1990	Bank of China Tower, Hong Kong
1991	One Canada Square, London
1992	Central Plaza, Hong Kong

Across the Nation

How many of these big national stories do you remember unfolding live on TV and radio?

- ✦ Model Cindy Crawford stars in Super Bowl Pepsi commercial
- ✦ North American Free Trade Agreement signed
- ✦ Hurricane Andrew hits the coast
- ✦ Bill Clinton elected president
- ✦ Space Shuttle Endeavor launched
- ✦ Mafia boss John Gotti sentenced to life imprisonment
- ✦ Great Chicago Flood strikes
- ✦ Cartoon Network begins broadcasting
- ✦ Mall of America opens for business
- ✦ TWA declares bankruptcy
- ✦ Riots occur after officers acquitted in Rodney King beating
- ✦ Microsoft releases Windows 3.1
- ✦ Video telephones become available
- ✦ Ross Perot becomes 3rd party nominee for president
- ✦ Four teen girls torture and murder another teen girl
- ✦ Washington Redskins win the Super Bowl
- ✦ Two large earthquakes hit California
- ✦ Ruby Ridge 11-day siege occurs when marshals serve warrant
- ✦ Peekskill meteorite destroys family's car
- ✦ Military leaves the Philippines after a base there for 100 years
- ✦ Bonnie Blair wins gold in 1992 Winter Olympics
- ✦ Three astronauts perform spacewalks at the same time
- ✦ Shipment of rubber ducks falls overboard (they'll float ashore for years)
- ✦ "You can't handle the truth" becomes a catchphrase

Born this year:
- ⚭ Singer Selena Gomez
- ⚭ Rapper Cardi B
- ⚭ Journalist Kaitlan Collins

Around the World When You Turned 50

(50)

Here is the last set of international headlines in the book, and they're not so long ago (comparatively speaking).

+ Yitzhak Rabin becomes Prime Minister
+ Bosnia Herzegovina declares independence
+ European Union becomes official
+ Turkey hit by earthquake
+ Sewer explosion kills hundreds in Mexico
+ Violence begins between Indian Hindus and Muslims
+ Euro Disney opens in Paris
+ Truck drivers protest in France
+ Spain hosts Summer Olympics
+ Afghanistan overthrows communist government
+ Prince Charles and Lady Di separate
+ Winter Games open in France
+ Japan officially apologizes to Korea for actions in WWII
+ Salvadoran Civil War ends
+ Elizabeth II marks 40 years of rule
+ Iraq defies UN over nuclear inspections
+ Coal mine collapses in Turkey
+ Pakistan wins Cricket World Cup
+ Strong earthquake hits Germany, Belgium, and the Netherlands
+ Military coup overthrows Sierra Leone government
+ UN peacekeepers leave Sarajevo
+ Giotto spacecraft takes sample of comet
+ UK prime minister announces Iraqi no-fly zones
+ Nicaragua hit by earthquake and tsunami
+ Leader of Shining Path is arrested in Peru
+ Prison massacre in Brazil
+ Church of England allows women to become priests
+ Czechoslovakia votes to split in two

Kentucky Derby Winners

These are the equine and human heroes from the "most exciting two minutes of sport" during your thirties and forties. Did any of them make you rich?

1972	Riva Ridge (Ron Turcotte)
1973	**Secretariat (Ron Turcotte)**

Secretariat and Sham, both racing in the 1973 Kentucky Derby, had what still stand as the two fastest times ever in the race. Secretariat broke the track records at all three Triple Crown races (Kentucky Derby, Preakness Stakes, Belmont Stakes).

1974	Cannonade (Angel Cordero Jr.)
1975	Foolish Pleasure (Jacinto Vasquez)
1976	Bold Forbes (Angel Cordero Jr.)
1977	Seattle Slew (Jean Cruguet)
1978	**Affirmed (Steve Cauthen)**

Affirmed won the Triple Crown, with Alydar finishing second in all three Triple Crown races.

1979	Spectacular Bid (Ronnie Franklin)
1980	**Genuine Risk (Jacinto Vasquez)**

Genuine Risk became the first female horse to win the Kentucky Derby since 1915.

1981	Pleasant Colony (Jorge Velasquez)
1982	Gato Del Sol (Eddie Delahoussaye)
1983	Sunny's Halo (Eddie Delahoussaye)
1984	Swale (Laffit Pincay Jr.)
1985	Spend A Buck (Angel Cordero Jr.)
1986	Ferdinand (Bill Shoemaker)
1987	Alysheba (Chris McCarron)
1988	Winning Colors (Gary Stevens)
1989	Sunday Silence (Pat Valenzuela)
1990	Unbridled (Craig Perret)
1991	Strike the Gold (Chris Antley)
1992	Lil E. Tee (Pat Day)

World Series Champions Since You Were Born

These are the winners of the Commissioner's Trophy and the number of times they've been victorious in your lifetime.

- Detroit Tigers (3)
- New York Yankees (18)
- Cincinnati Reds (3)
- St. Louis Cardinals (7)
- Cleveland Indians (1)
- New York Giants (1)
- Brooklyn Dodgers (1)
- Milwaukee Braves (1)
- **Los Angeles Dodgers (6)**
  1988: Dodgers' Kirk Gibson, battling injuries, hit a game-winning home run in his only at-bat of the 1988 World Series.
- Pittsburgh Pirates (3)
- Baltimore Orioles (3)
- **New York Mets (2)**
  1969: The Mets had never finished above 9th in their division.
- Oakland Athletics (4)
- Philadelphia Phillies (2)
- Kansas City Royals (2)
- **Minnesota Twins (2)**
  1991: Both teams had finished in last place the previous season.
- Toronto Blue Jays (2)
- Atlanta Braves (2)
- Florida Marlins (2)
- Arizona Diamondbacks (1)
- Anaheim Angels (1)
- Boston Red Sox (4)
- Chicago White Sox (1)
- San Francisco Giants (3)
- **Chicago Cubs (1)**
  2016: The Cubs' first World Series win since 1908.
- Houston Astros (1)
- Washington Nationals (1)

Books of the Decade

By our forties, most of us have decided what we like to read. But occasionally a book can break the spell, revealing the delights of other genres. Did any of these newly published books do that for you?

1982	The Color Purple by Alice Walker
1982	Space by James A. Michener
1983	Pet Sematary by Stephen King
1983	Hollywood Wives by Jackie Collins
1984	You Can Heal Your Life by Louise Hay
1984	Money: A Suicide Note by Martin Amis
1985	The Handmaid's Tale by Margaret Atwood
1985	White Noise by Don DeLillo
1985	Lake Wobegon Days by Garrison Keillor
1986	It by Stephen King
1986	Wanderlust by Danielle Steele
1987	Patriot Games by Tom Clancy
1987	Beloved by Toni Morrison
1987	The Bonfire of the Vanities by Tom Wolfe
1988	The Cardinal of the Kremlin by Tom Clancy
1988	The Sands of Time by Sidney Sheldon
1989	Clear and Present Danger by Stephen R. Covey
1989	The Pillars of the Earth by Ken Follett
1990	The Plains of Passage by Jean M. Auel
1990	Possession by A.S. Byatt
1990	Four Past Midnight by Stephen King
1991	The Firm by John Grisham
1991	The Kitchen God's Wife by Amy Tan
1991	Scarlett by Alexandra Ripley

Vice Presidents in Your Lifetime

The linchpin of a successful presidency, the best springboard to become POTUS, or both? Here are the men—and woman—who have shadowed the most powerful person in the world in your lifetime.

1941–45	Henry A. Wallace
1945	Harry S. Truman
1949–53	**Alben W. Barkley** He died of a heart attack during a speech at a political convention three years after the end of his term.
1953–61	Richard Nixon
1961–63	Lyndon B. Johnson
1965–69	Hubert Humphrey
1969–73	**Spiro Agnew (right)**
1973–74	Gerald Ford
1974–77	Nelson Rockefeller
1977–81	Walter Mondale
1981–89	**George H. W. Bush** He is only the second vice president to win the presidency while holding the office of vice president.
1989–93	**Dan Quayle** Quayle famously misspelled potato ("potatoe")
1993–2001	**Al Gore** This VP won the Nobel Peace Prize in 2007, following in the footsteps of two other former vice presidents.
2001–09	Dick Cheney
2009–17	Joe Biden
2017–20	**Mike Pence** In the 90s, Pence took a break from politics to become a conservative radio talk show and television host.
2020–	Kamala Harris

Spiro Agnew resigned in 1973, the second VP to quit in America's history (the first was John Calhoun in 1932). He stepped down after being charged with tax evasion and taking bribes. He covered his legal debts with a loan from friend Frank Sinatra. In 1983 he was compelled to repay $268,000: the money he had taken in bribes, plus interest.

British Prime Ministers in Your Lifetime

These are the occupants of 10 Downing Street, London, during your lifetime (not including Larry the resident cat). The list features two women, three knights, and two who returned for a second go.

1940–45	Winston Churchill
1945–51	Clement Attlee
1951–55	**Sir Winston Churchill**
	Churchill was made an honorary citizen of the United States in 1963, one of only eight to receive this honor.
1955–57	Sir Anthony Eden
1957–63	**Harold Macmillan**
	Macmillan was the scion of a wealthy publishing family. He resigned following a scandal in which a minister was found to have lied about his relationship with a 19-year-old model. Macmillan died aged 92; his last words were, "I think I will go to sleep now."
1963–64	Sir Alec Douglas-Home
1964–70	Harold Wilson
1970–74	Edward Heath
1974–76	Harold Wilson
1976–79	James Callaghan
1979–90	**Margaret Thatcher**
	In 1994, Thatcher was working late in a Brighton hotel, preparing a conference speech. A bomb—planted weeks earlier by the IRA five stories above—detonated, devastating the hotel. Five were killed; Thatcher was unscathed. The conference went ahead.
1990–97	John Major
1997–2007	Tony Blair
2007–10	Gordon Brown
2010–16	David Cameron
2016–19	Theresa May
2019–	Boris Johnson

Things People Do Now (Part 2)

Imagine your ten-year-old self being given this list of today's mundane tasks and habits—and the puzzled look on your face!

+ Listen to a podcast
+ Go "viral" or become social media famous
+ Watch YouTube
+ Track the exact location of family members via your smartphone
+ Watch college football playoffs
+ Have drive-thru fast food delivered to your door
+ Check reviews before trying a new restaurant or product
+ Use LED light bulbs to save on your electric bill
+ Wear leggings as pants for any occasion
+ Use hashtags (#) to express an idea or show support
+ Join a CrossFit gym
+ Use a Forever stamp to send a letter
+ Carry a reusable water bottle
+ Work for a company with an "unlimited" paid time off policy
+ "Binge" a TV show
+ Marry a person of the same sex
+ Take your shoes off when going through airport security
+ Take a selfie
+ Use tooth-whitening strips
+ Feed babies and kids from food pouches
+ Buy recreational marijuana from a dispensary (in some states)
+ Store documents "in the cloud" and work on them from any device
+ Clean up after your pets using compostable waste bags
+ Buy free-range eggs and meat at the grocery store

A Lifetime of Technology

It's easy to lose sight of the breadth and volume of life-enhancing technology that became commonplace during the 20th Century. Here are some of the most notable advances to be made in the years you've been an adult.

1963	**Computer mouse** The inventor of the computer mouse patented it in 1963. However, by the time the mouse became commercially available in the 1980s, his patent had expired.
1969	Laser printer
1971	Email
1972	Video games console (Magnavox Odyssey)
1973	Mobile phone
1974	Universal Product Code
1979	Compact disc
1982	**Emoticons** The inventor of the smiley emoticon hands out "Smiley" cookies every September 19th—the anniversary of the first time it was used.
1983	Internet
1986	Mir Space Station
1988	**Internet virus** The first Internet worm was specifically designed to crack passwords. Its inventor was the son of the man who invented computer passwords.
1989	World Wide Web
1992	Digital hand-sized mobile phone
1995	**Mouse with scroll wheel** Mouse scroll wheels were developed primarily as a zoom function for large Excel sheets, but became more useable as a means of scrolling.
1998	Google
1999	Wi-Fi
2000	Camera phone
2001	Wikipedia
2004	Facebook
2007	Apple iPhone
2009	Bitcoin

The Biggest Hits When You Were 50

Fifty: an age when your musical taste is largely settled and modern music can lose its appeal...but how many do you know and how many do you like?

Prince and the
New Power Generation 🎵 Diamonds and Pearls
Whitney Houston 🎵 I Will Always Love You
Right Said Fred 🎵 I'm Too Sexy
Nirvana 🎵 Come As You Are
Brooks and Dunn 🎵 Boot Scootin' Boogie
Michael Jackson 🎵 Remember the Time
Mr. Big 🎵 To Be with You
Mary Chapin Carpenter 🎵 I Feel Lucky
Boyz II Men 🎵 End of the Road
Eric Clapton 🎵 Tears in Heaven
Snap! 🎵 Rhythm Is a Dancer
Billy Ray Cyrus 🎵 Achy Breaky Heart
En Vogue 🎵 My Lovin'
(You're Never Gonna Get It)
Guns N' Roses 🎵 December Rain
Tom Cochrane 🎵 Life Is a Highway
Diamond Rio 🎵 Norma Jean Riley
Sophie B. Hawkins 🎵 Damn I Wish I Was Your Lover
U2 🎵 One
Mary J. Blige 🎵 Real Love
The Heights 🎵 How Do You Talk to an Angel
Genesis 🎵 I Can't Dance
Red Hot Chili Peppers 🎵 Under the Bridge
The Cure 🎵 Friday I'm in Love
TLC 🎵 Ain't 2 Proud 2 Beg

Grand Constructions

Governments around the world spent much of the 20th century nation building (and rebuilding), with huge civil engineering projects employing new construction techniques. Here are some of the biggest built between the ages of 25 and 50.

1967	Lion Rock Tunnel, Hong Kong
1968	Nanjing Yangtze River Bridge, China
1970	Flathead Tunnel, US
1971	Azadi Tower, Iran
1972	Snowy Mountains Scheme, Australia
1973	Chesapeake Bay Bridge, US
1974	Charles de Gaulle Airport, France
1975	Orange-Fish River Tunnel, South Africa
1976	**Sonnenberg Tunnel, Switzerland**

A 5,000-ft road tunnel built to double up as a 20,000-capacity nuclear shelter. Blast doors weigh 350 tons... but take 24 hours to close.

1977	Guoliang Tunnel, China
1978	West Gate Bridge, Australia
1979	Genting Sempah Tunnel, Malaysia
1980	Reichsbrücke, Austria
1981	Tjörn Bridge, Scandanavia
1982	Abu Dhabi International Airport, Abu Dhabi
1983	Queen Alia International Airport, Jordan
1984	Tennessee-Tombigbee Waterway, US
1985	Penang Bridge, Malaysia
1986	National Waterway 1, India
1987	Pikeville Cut-Through, US
1988	Great Seto Bridge, Japan
1989	Skybridge (TransLink), Canada
1990	Ningbo Lishe International Airport, China
1991	Fannefjord Tunnel, Norway
1992	Vidyasagar Setu Bridge, India

Popular Food in the 1980s

The showy eighties brought us food to dazzle and delight. Food to make us feel good, food to share and food to go. Some innovations fell by the wayside, but many more can still be found in our baskets forty years later.

Hot Pockets
Hot Pockets were the brainchild of two brothers, originally from Iran. Their invention was launched as the Tastywich before being tweaked to become the Hot Pockets enjoyed by millions.

Bagel Bites

Crystal Light

Steak-Umms

Sizzlean Bacon

Potato skins appetizers

Tofutti ice cream

Hi-C Ecto Cooler
Hi-C has been around for a very long time, but the Ecto Cooler dates back to the Ghostbusters movie hype of the 1980s.

Hot buttered O's

Knorr Spinach Dip

Original New York Seltzer

Blondies

Blackened Redfish
The trend for blackening redfish prompted fish stocks to drop so low that commercial fishing for the species was banned in Louisiana.

Bartles & Jaymes Wine Coolers

Fruit Wrinkles

Stuffed mushrooms appetizers

TCBY Frozen Yogurt
TCBY originally stood for "This Can't Be Yogurt."

Sushi

Fajitas

Capri Sun

Jell-O Pudding Pops

Lean Cuisine frozen meals
Lean Cuisine is an FDA-regulated term, so all Lean Cuisine frozen meals need to be within the limit for saturated fat and cholesterol.

Eighties Symbols of Success

In the flamboyant era of Dallas and Dynasty there were many ways to show that you, too, had really made it. Forty years on, it's fascinating to see how some of these throwbacks are outdated or available to nearly everyone, while others are still reserved for today's wealthy peacocks.

BMW car

Cellular car phone

Rolex watch

Cosmetic surgery

In 1981 there were 1,000 liposuction procedures performed. That number increased to 250,000 by 1989.

VCR

"Home theater" projection TV

In-ground pool

AKC-registered dog

McMansion

Pagers/"beeper"

Aprica stroller

Home intercom system

Heart-shaped Jacuzzi tub

NordicTrack

This machine was originally called the Nordic Jock but was renamed due to compaints from women's rights groups.

Cruise vacation

Restaurant-standard kitchen appliances

A popular commercial stove produced enough heat to warm an average three-bedroom home. It was the energy equivalent of six residential stoves.

Ronald Reagan-style crystal jelly bean jar on your desk

Apple or Commodore 64 home computer

Volvo Station Wagon

Gordon Gekko-style "power suit"

Owning a horse or riding lessons for your children

Private jet

Tennis bracelet

Monogrammed clothes and accessories

Launched in 1980, the Apple III personal computer seen here went on sale for a hefty $4,000 and up, the equivalent of over $13,000 today. It didn't sell well and was soon withdrawn (unlike the Apple II, which went on to sell more than 5 million units).

The Transportation Coils

This novel issue of more than 50 definitive stamps first appeared on post in the early eighties, and became a favorite of collectors for its mono color engraved images of transportation methods past and present. Stamps carrying the printing plate number are particularly treasured. Here's a selection you may remember.

1 c 🖾 Omnibus
2 c 🖾 Locomotive
3 c 🖾 Handcar
4 c 🖾 **Stagecoach**

Coaches have been ferrying people and mail between US towns and cities since the late 18th century.

5 c 🖾 Motorcycle
5.5c 🖾 **Star Route Truck**

Star routes were 19th century mail routes on which carriers bid to make deliveries.

6 c 🖾 Tricycle
7.4 c 🖾 Baby Buggy
10 c 🖾 Canal Boat
11 c 🖾 Caboose
12.5 c 🖾 Pushcart
13 c 🖾 Patrol Wagon
15 c 🖾 Tugboat
17 c 🖾 Electric Auto
17 c 🖾 Dog Sled
17.5 c 🖾 Racing car
18 c 🖾 Surrey
20 c 🖾 Cog Railway
21 c 🖾 Railway Mail Car
23 c 🖾 Lunch Wagon
24.1 c 🖾 Tandem Bike
25 c 🖾 Bread Wagon
32 c 🖾 Ferry Boat
$1 🖾 **Sea Plane**

The US Navy bought its first sea plane in 1911: a Curtiss Model E, with a range of 150 miles.

Eighties Game Shows

By the eighties, game shows had their work cut out to compete against the popularity of new drama and talk shows. Still, an injection of celebrity glamour and dollar bills—alongside hours to be filled on new cable TV channels—ensured their survival. Here are the biggies.

Double Dare 🎬 (1986-2019)
Remote Control 🎬 (1987-90)
Scrabble 🎬 (1984-93)
The Price Is Right 🎬 (1972-present)
"Come on down!"—perhaps the best-known game show catchphrase of all time. One 2008 contestant was even happier than usual to do just that after 3 chips dropped into the Plinko all hit the $10,000 jackpot. Fluke? No, wires used to rig the result when filming ads hadn't been removed. She was allowed to keep the $30,000.

Family Feud 🎬 (1976-present)
Press Your Luck 🎬 (1983-86)
A show perhaps best remembered for the contestant Michael Larson, who memorized the game board and engineered a winning streak worth over $110,000. It wasn't cheating—Larson kept the winnings—but the game was swiftly reformulated.

Chain Reaction 🎬 1980-present)
Blockbusters 🎬 (1980-87)
Win, Lose, or Draw 🎬 (1987-90)
On The Spot 🎬 (1984-88)
Jeopardy! 🎬 (1964-present)
Card Sharks 🎬 (1978-present)
Wheel of Fortune 🎬 (1975-present)
Hostess Vanna White is estimated to clap 600 times a show; that's around 4,000,000 times since she began in 1982.

Fandango 🎬 (1983-88)
Body Language 🎬 (1984-86)
Jackpot! 🎬 (1974-90)

Popular Boys' Names

Not many of these boys' names were popular when you were born. But how many more of them are now in your twenty-first century family?

Jacob

Michael

Joshua

Joshua is very much a turn-of-the-century kind of name. He entered the Top 100 in 1972 and climbed to spend 25 years inside the top 5; now, he rarely makes the top 50.

Matthew

Ethan

Andrew

Joseph

Christopher

Nicholas

Daniel

William

Anthony

David

Tyler

Alexander

Ryan

John

James

Zachary

Brandon

Jonathan

Justin

Dylan

Christian

Samuel

Austin

Rising and falling stars:

Dominic, Jaden, Owen, Hayden, Diego and Riley are in; Jared, Garrett, Mark, Jeremy and Bryce are out.

Popular Girls' Names

60 It's a similar story for girls' names: only Elizabeth featured in the 30 most popular names for your year of birth. How long will it be before we turn full circle and Shirley, Patricia and Barbara make a comeback?

Emily
Emily has held the top slot for 12 years since 1900—more than most. Though nobody comes close to Mary (54 years). Others: Linda (6), Lisa (8), Jennifer (15), Jessica (9), Ashley (2), Emma (6), Isabella (2), Sophia (3) and Olivia (since 2019).

Madison
Hannah
Emma
Alexis
Ashley
Abigail
Sarah
Samantha
Olivia
Elizabeth
Alyssa
Lauren
Isabella
Grace
Jessica
Brianna
Taylor
Kayla
Anna
Victoria
Megan
Sydney
Rachel

Rising and falling stars:
Say hello to Riley, Lily, Ava, Maya and Jocelyn; wave goodbye to Angela, Courtney and Christina.

Game Show Hosts of the Seventies and Eighties

Here is the new generation of hosts: bow-tied, wide-smiled men to steer family favorites through tumultuous times. Astonishingly, one or two are still holding the cards.

John Charles Daly ⋈ What's My Line (1950–1967)
Garry Moore ⋈ To Tell The Truth (1969–1976)
Chuck Woolery ⋈ Love Connection (1983–1994)
Bob Barker ⋈ The Price Is Right (1972–2007)
Pat Sajak ⋈ Wheel of Fortune (1981–)
Sajak took the crown for the longest-reigning game-show host of all time in 1983, when his 35-year reign surpassed that of Bob Barker as host of The Price is Right.

Peter Tomarken ⋈ Press Your Luck (1983–86)
Gene Rayburn ⋈ The Match Game (1962–1981)
Alex Trebek ⋈ Jeopardy! (1984–2020)
At the time of his death in 2020, Trebek had hosted more than 8,200 episodes of the show.

Dick Clark ⋈ Pyramid (1973–1988)
Richard Dawson ⋈ Family Feud (1976–1995)
Peter Marshall ⋈ Hollywood Squares (1966–1981)
Howard Cosell ⋈ Battle of the Network Stars (1976–1988)
Marc Summers ⋈ Double Dare (1986–1993)
Tom Kennedy ⋈ Name That Tune (1974–1981)
Bert Convy ⋈ Tattletales (1974–78; 1982–84)
Ken Ober ⋈ Remote Control (1987–1990)
Jim Lange ⋈ The Dating Game (1965–1980)
Wink Martindale ⋈ Tic-Tac-Dough (1978–1985)
Art Fleming ⋈ Jeopardy! (1964–1975; 1978–79)
Host for the original version, Fleming declined to host the comeback in 1983. His friend Pat Sajak took the job.

Jack Narz ⋈ Concentration (1973–78)
Dennis James ⋈ The Price Is Right (1972–77)
Jim Perry ⋈ $ale of the Century (1983–89)
John Davidson ⋈ Hollywood Squares (1986–89)
Ray Combs ⋈ Family Feud (1988–1994)
Mike Adamle ⋈ American Gladiators (1989–1996)

TV News Anchors of the Seventies and Eighties

The explosion in cable channels that began with CNN in 1980 brought a host of fresh presenters to join the ranks of trusted personalities that bring us the news. How many of them do you remember?

Dan Rather ♟ (CBS)
"Kenneth, what's the frequency?" Those were the words of the man who attacked Rather in 1986. It took a decade before the message was decoded; his assailant wanted to block the beams he believed TV networks were using to target him.

Peter Jennings ♟ (ABC)
Tom Brokaw ♟ (NBC)
Ted Koppel ♟ (ABC)
Bill Beutel ♟ (ABC)
Jessica Savitch ♟ (NBC)
Connie Chung ♟ (NBC)
Diane Sawyer ♟ (CBS/ABC)
Sam Donaldson ♟ (ABC)
Barbara Walters ♟ (ABC)
Walters was a popular pioneer; the first woman to co-host and anchor news programs, reaching 74 million viewers with her interview of Monica Lewinsky.

Frank Reynolds ♟ (ABC)
Jane Pauley ♟ (NBC)
Roger Grimsby ♟ (ABC)
Roger Mudd ♟ (CBS/NBC)
Garrick Utley ♟ (NBC)
Bernard Shaw ♟ (CNN)
Frank McGee ♟ (NBC)
Ed Bradley ♟ (CBS)
Larry King ♟ (CNN)
Kathleen Sullivan ♟ (ABC/CBS/NBC)
Jim Lehrer ♟ (PBS)
Robert MacNeil ♟ (PBS)
In 1963, MacNeil had a brief exchange of words with a man leaving the Texas School Book Depository; to this day, it is uncertain whether this was Lee Harvey Oswald.

FIFA World Cup: Down to the Last Four in Your Life

Here are the teams that have made the last four of the world's most watched sporting event in your lifetime (last year in brackets). The US men's team has reached the semifinals once, back in 1930.

France ⚽ (2018, winner)

Croatia ⚽ (2018, runner-up)

During a 2006 match against Australia, Croatian player Josip Šimunić was booked three times due to a referee blunder.

Belgium ⚽ (2018, 3rd)

England ⚽ (2018, 4th)

In the run-up to the 1966 World Cup, hosted and won by England, the trophy was held to ransom. An undercover detective with fake banknotes arrested the crook; a dog named Pickles found the trophy under a bush.

Brazil ⚽ (2014, 4th)

Germany ⚽ (2014, winner)

Argentina ⚽ (2014, runner-up)

Netherlands ⚽ (2014, 3rd)

Spain ⚽ (2010, winner)

Uruguay ⚽ (2010, 4th)

Italy ⚽ (2006, winner)

Portugal ⚽ (2006, 4th)

Turkey ⚽ (2002, 3rd)

Korean Republic ⚽ (2002, 4th)

Sweden ⚽ (1994, 3rd)

Bulgaria ⚽ (1994, 4th)

Poland ⚽ (1982, 3rd)

Russia ⚽ (1966, 4th)

Czech Republic (as Czechoslovakia) ⚽ (1962, runner-up)

Chile ⚽ (1962, 3rd)

The 1962 World Cup saw the 'Battle of Santiago' between Chile and Italy. The first foul occurred 12 seconds into the game, a player was punched in the nose, and police intervened several times.

Serbia (as Yugoslavia) ⚽ (1962, 4th)

Hungary ⚽ (1954, runner-up)

Austria ⚽ (1954, third)

Books of the Decade

Our final decade of books are the bookstore favorites from your fifties. How many did you read...and can you remember the plot, or the cover?

1992	The Bridges of Madison County by Robert James Waller
1992	The Secret History by Donna Tartt
1993	The Celestine Prophecy by James Redfield
1993	Like Water for Chocolate by Laura Esquivel
1994	The Chamber by John Grisham
1994	Disclosure by Michael Crichton
1995	The Horse Whisperer by Nicholas Evans
1995	The Lost World by Michael Crichton
1995	The Rainmaker by John Grisham
1996	Angela's Ashes by Frank McCourt
1996	Bridget Jones's Diary by Helen Fielding
1996	Infinite Jest by David Foster Wallace
1997	American Pastoral by Philip Roth
1997	Tuesdays with Morrie by Mitch Albom
1998	The Poisonwood Bible by Barbara Kingsolver
1998	A Man in Full by Tom Wolfe
1999	The Testament by John Grisham
1999	Hannibal by Thomas Harris
1999	Girl with a Pearl Earring by Tracy Chevalier
2000	Angels & Demons by Dan Brown
2000	Interpreter of Maladies by Jhumpa Lahiri
2000	White Teeth by Zadie Smith
2001	Life of Pi by Yann Martel
2001	The Corrections by Jonathan Franzen

April 17, 1970: Jim Lovell is brought aboard a helicopter—the last of the
three astronauts from the Apollo 13 mission to be lifted from the floating

Apollo Astronauts

Whatever your personal memories of the events, the moon landings are now woven into our national story—but not all of the Apollo astronauts who made the journey are equally well known. Twelve landed; twelve remained in lunar orbit. Gus Grissom, Ed White, and Roger B Chaffee died in training.

Landed on the moon:

Alan Bean

Alan Shepard
Shepard was the oldest person to walk on the moon at age 47.

Buzz Aldrin

Charles Duke

David Scott

Edgar Mitchell

Eugene Cernan

Harrison Schmitt

James Irwin

John Young

Neil Armstrong

Pete Conrad

Remained in low orbit:

Al Worden

Bill Anders
Anders took the iconic "Earthrise" photo.

Dick Gordon

Frank Borman

Fred Haise

Jack Swigert

Jim Lovell

Ken Mattingly

Michael Collins

Ron Evans
Made the final spacewalk of the program to retrieve film cassettes.

Stuart Roosa
On the Apollo 14 mission he carried seeds from 5 species of trees. They were planted across the US and are known as "Moon Trees."

Tom Stafford

US Open Tennis

And now it's the women's turn. ...e are the tournament's victors when you were between the ages of the current "winning window": 16 years (Tracy Austin in 1979), and a venerable 42 years (Molla Mallory in 1926: she won eight times).

1957-58	**Althea Gibson** Gibson became the first black US Open winner.
1959	Maria Bueno
1960-61	Darlene Hard
1962	Margaret Court
1963-64	Maria Bueno
1965	Margaret Court
1966	Maria Bueno
1967	Billie Jean King
1968	Virginia Wade
1969-70	Margaret Court
1971-72	Billie Jean King
1973	**Margaret Court** In 1973, the US Open became the first Grand Slam tournament to offer equal prize money to male and female winners.
1974	Billie Jean King
1975-78	**Chris Evert** During the 1975 US Open, Evert beat her long-time rival Martina Navratilova in the semi-final. That evening, Navratilova defected to the United States and subsequently won the US Open four times.
1979	**Tracy Austin** 16-year-old Tracy Austin is the youngest US Open champion ever.
1980	Chris Evert
1981	Tracy Austin
1982	Chris Evert
1983-84	Martina Navratilova

The Biggest Hits When You Were 60

We're not reaching back very far for these hits—but unless you're very young at heart, that probably means you won't know very many of them!

Nickelback How You Remind me

Puddle of Mudd Blurry

Eminem Without Me

The Dixie Chicks Long Time Gone

Kylie Minogue Can't Get You Out of My Head

LeAnn Rimes Can't Fight the Moonlight

Ashanti Foolish

Red Hot Chili Peppers Can't Stop

Kenny Chesney The Good Stuff

Jewel Standing Still

3 Doors Down When I'm Gone

The Soggy Bottom Boys I Am a Man of Constant Sorrow

Nelly featuring Kelly Rowland Dilemma

The Calling Wherever You Will Go

Rascal Flatts I'm Movin' On

Pink Don't Let Me Get Me

John Mayer No Such Thing

Martina McBride Blesses

No Doubt Hey Baby

Michelle Branch All You Wanted

Creed My Sacrifice

Diamond Rio Beautiful Mess

Mary J. Blige Family Affair

Five for Fighting Superman (It's Not Easy)

Things People Did When You Were Growing Up (Part 2)

Finally, here are more of the things we did and errands we ran as kids that nobody needs, wants, or even understands how to do in the modern age!

+ Buy cigarettes for your parents at the corner store as a child
+ Use a pay phone (there was one on almost every corner)
+ Join a bowling league
+ Collect cigarette or baseball trading cards
+ Get frozen meals delivered to your door by the iconic refrigerated yellow Schwan's truck
+ Attend "Lawn Faiths"/ ice cream socials
+ Chat with strangers over CB radio
+ Look up a phone number in the Yellow or White Pages
+ Visit the Bookmobile for new library books
+ Have a radio repaired at an appliance/electronics shop
+ Ride your bike without a helmet
+ Go to American Bandstand parties
+ Take part in a panty raid prank
+ Attend a sock hop
+ Get milk delivered to your door
+ Hang out with friends at a pizzeria
+ Use a rotary phone at home
+ Use a typewriter
+ Save your term paper on a floppy disc
+ Listen to LPs and the newest 45s
+ Care for a pet rock
+ Use a card catalogue to find books at the library
+ Attend a Sadie Hawkins Dance where girls invited the boys
+ Go disco roller skating

Made in the USA
Monee, IL
21 November 2022

18260335R10067